IMAGES
of America

THE CHICAGO OUTFIT

Al Capone is standing in court, with the famous scars on the left side of his face and neck showing.

IMAGES
of America

THE CHICAGO OUTFIT

John J. Binder

ARCADIA
PUBLISHING

Published by Arcadia Publishing
Charleston, South Carolina

Printed in the United States of America

Library of Congress Catalog Card Number: 2003101080

For all general information contact Arcadia Publishing at:
Telephone 843-853-2070
Fax 843-853-0044
E-mail sales@arcadiapublishing.com
For customer service and orders:
Toll-Free 1-888-313-2665

Visit us on the Internet at www.arcadiapublishing.com

To my family.

CONTENTS

The victim of this typical gangland hit was dumped in the street, probably from a moving car in which the actual shooting had occurred.

ACKNOWLEDGMENTS

I am grateful to Bill Balsamo, Larry Bergreen, Bill Brashler, Mars Eghigian, Jolene Emery, Mel Holli, Wayne Johnson, Gary Linden, Mark Levell, Robert "Mickey" Lombardo, Jim McGuire, David Olster, Chuck Schauer, Hank Scheafer, Bob Schoenberg, the people at the University of Illinois at Chicago photo lab and the staff of the Chicago Crime Commission for their comments and assistance at various times. Special thanks are owed to Art Bilek, Matt Luzi and Jeff Thurston, three individuals who possess a wealth of knowledge about organized crime in Chicago and have freely shared it with me, as well as various well informed people who spoke to me on the condition of anonymity. Readers interested in the Chicago Outfit may contact the author at wsidejack@yahoo.com.

INTRODUCTION

Many people in Chicago and elsewhere, myself included, are intrigued by the history of organized crime in the city and the surrounding areas. This book is an outgrowth of that interest. After more than a decade of serious research on the subject (and collecting related photos), I have pulled together various materials to tell the story of the Chicago Outfit in words and pictures.

It is a fascinating story, both because organized crime has greatly influenced the history of the city and because the complete story has not been told in print. To see the influence of the Chicago Mob on the city, one need look no further than Len O'Connor's book *Clout* or Ovid Demaris's *Captive City*, which detail how the hoodlums received not only extensive political protection allowing them to operate but at one time actually controlled the political apparatus in various wards in the city as well as individual judges, legislators, and congressmen. Yet, although much has already been written on organized crime in Chicago, there is no full history of the Outfit. Previous books focus on specific individuals, such as Al Capone, Eliot Ness, or Tony Accardo, or specific time periods—for example, Prohibition or through about 1970—but they do not explain where the Outfit came from, what its activities have been during various periods, how and why the organization has changed over time from its inception to the present day, or what factors caused its incredible rise and decline.

To begin at the beginning, what is the "Outfit"? In one respect it is the label generally used to refer to the organized crime family (organization) in Chicago. This name for the Chicago Mob seems to have first appeared as a proper noun in the early 1950s and became popular some time later. In terms of who and what they are, the Outfit is a criminal enterprise, organized for the profit of its members, which is part of the Cosa Nostra in the United States. It has dominated organized crime in and around Chicago, as well as in certain other parts of the country, since the end of Prohibition. In terms of business activities, over time the Outfit has been extremely successful, more so than any other group of organized criminals in the country.

Notice that I do *not* refer to the Outfit as part of the Mafia. There is no Mafia boss of Chicago. Furthermore, there is no Mafia boss of the United States (based supposedly in New York) who the Chicago Mafia boss reports to, nor is there a boss of the international Mafia in Sicily who the United States boss reports to. The Mafia is in Sicily—and only Sicily. It is made up of Sicilians. In the United States we have our own, unique form of organized crime, which, although it has had many members of Sicilian or Italian extraction, is much more ethnically diverse than the organized crime found in Italy.

The Cosa Nostra is an affiliation of the various gangs in the major cities that arose during Prohibition. It is a loose affiliation. The individual gangs co-operate through a national commission (or at least have in the past), of which Chicago has always been a member, which settles inter-city matters. But there is no "Boss of Bosses" of the Cosa Nostra who gives orders to the various gangs (commonly referred to as "families") in the various cities. At least not since New York's Salvatore Maranzano tried to assume that title in 1931 and was thoroughly perforated by gunmen sent by Lucky Luciano. Rather, each major gang has its own boss who directs the group's operations in its own geographical area(s).

It bears repeating that the Outfit's main focus, like other organized crime families, is on making its members wealthier. The violence committed by the Outfit and its predecessors in Chicago, although it is extremely fascinating to many average citizens, as well as writers and Hollywood film producers, is secondary to the whole process. Because the Chicago Mob is involved in criminal activities, it does not (as opposed to a legitimate business) use legal means to settle its disputes with people. Instead it uses violence to persuade and punish. And the Outfit can be extremely violent, even in comparison to other Cosa Nostra families. Similarly, political power is not an objective of the Outfit. Rather, it is a tool used to further their business activities and to protect the members.

All that having been said, let us go back to the era before Prohibition to begin the story of the Outfit and explore its successes and failures, as well as the reasons behind both.

One

IN THE BEGINNING

The story of the Outfit begins with James "Big Jim" Colosimo. Before Colosimo, organized crime in Chicago was generally small in scale and specialized. One group of people controlled individual, or usually at most two, labor unions. Another group was active in gambling, such as Mike McDonald who was also a power in the Democratic Party. A third crowd was involved in prostitution, the largest of the three activities and one that made Chicago rather infamous, which was centered in the area just south of the downtown. But the trinity rarely, if ever, met.

From a modest start in the 1890s, Colosimo became Chicago's most powerful gangster during the period before Prohibition. He had superb political connections, first serving as a precinct captain in the organization of First Ward aldermen Coughlin and Kenna, and later becoming their bagman, making the collections related to prostitution in the red light district known as the Levee around 22nd and Dearborn. After 1915, "Big Jim" Colosimo directly received his political protection from Mayor William Hale Thompson's office in City Hall.

Colosimo built an empire centered around vice, but was involved in gambling and labor racketeering as well. When the public attitude turned against the idea of geographically segregated vice districts and authorities clamped down hard on the Levee, he opened new operations in various suburbs, in some cases far beyond the city limits. As Colosimo's holdings grew, so did his gang. By the mid-1910s he commanded Chicago's largest and strongest group of racketeers, including second in command John Torrio, who arrived from New York around 1909. This was a multi-ethnic gang, with Italian, Jewish, Irish, Greek, and other members. Colosimo's organization is the lineal ancestor of the gang led by Al Capone during Prohibition and the later Outfit, Capone himself having come to Chicago around 1919.

Jim Colosimo seemed reluctant, however, to pursue the rich opportunities in the liquor trade that Prohibition offered. Perhaps he was consumed with his young bride and his upscale restaurant, known as Colosimo's Café. When he returned from his honeymoon in May 1920 he was shot and killed at the café, most probably by New York gangster Frankie Yale under contract from John Torrio. Certainly, there are no hints of conflicts with other gangs at the time or reprisals carried out by Torrio et al., indicating that his own associates decided that Big Jim, who stood in the way of millions of dollars of wealth, had to go.

The far-sighted Torrio took over what Colosimo had built and used it as the foundation for a bootlegging empire. He is credited with calling together the other major local gangs in the very early days of Prohibition and forging them into a cartel that divided up the liquor business in the city in order to bring stability and maximum profitability to bootlegging. Each gang had a geographic area allocated to it and had the sole right, as agreed to by the cartel members, to sell beer and hard liquor in that area. The other major gangs in Chicago at the time included the

North Siders (generally east of the north branch of the Chicago River), led by Dion O'Banion, the Genna Brothers on the near West Side (around Taylor Street), the West Side O'Donnells (on the heavily Irish West Side), the Druggan-Lake gang (on the Near Southwest Side and west of there), the Saltis-McErlane gang (by the stockyards), and the Sheldon gang (in the South Side Irish belt, just east of Saltis and McErlane), which was originally united with the forces under Joe Saltis and Frank McErlane.

Torrio quickly gained an interest in several breweries, which gave him a reliable source of beer. He also developed or expanded operations in suburbs such as Burnham, South Chicago, Posen, Blue Island, Burr Oak, Stickney, and Forest View, in many cases following on the bordellos opened under Colosimo around World War I by introducing more brothels and controlling bootlegging. Torrio had the largest area in the cartel arrangement, covering the South Side (roughly the part of the city south of Madison Street and east of the current Dan Ryan expressway, with the exception of the district in the middle controlled by Ralph Sheldon) and areas south and west of the city.

Like all cartel agreements it faced trouble from without and from within. In the first case, people not included in the cartel naturally wanted to get a piece of the highly profitable pie. The first interlopers were the South Side O'Donnell gang, led by Edward "Spike" O'Donnell and containing several of his brothers, who tried to break into the Saltis-McErlane-Sheldon provinces in 1923. An inter-gang crew of gunmen from the "Combination" shot up the O'Donnell boys until they retreated back to south of 63rd Street and established themselves there for the rest of Prohibition.

The second problem was a much more difficult one. The group's profits would be the largest if everyone stuck to the agreement and stayed in their district. But any one gang could increase its own profits by cheating on the agreement and entering the territory of its neighbors. Friction between the Gennas and the O'Banion gang, which was perhaps inevitable given the large Sicilian neighborhood (at that time) along Division Street (centered east of Halsted) in the heart of the O'Banion area, sparked a general problem between the largely non-Italian North Siders and the various Italians. This led to the killing of O'Banion in November 1924, probably by Frankie Yale and two Genna gunmen, igniting the Prohibition-Era gang wars, referred to as the "Beer Wars" by old-time Chicago police officers.

Tall, dark, and squarely built, "Big Jim" Colosimo laid the foundation for those that came after him. His multiethnic organized crime conglomerate served as the blueprint for the Torrio-Capone Mob and the Outfit.

Colosimo's Restaurant at 2122 S Wabash was nationally renowned, serving millionaires, prostitutes and politicians alike. Big Jim was shot just inside the door to the right.

This previously unknown photo, taken before 1915, contains the hierarchy of Italian organized crime in Chicago and police officers from the 22nd Street station (in the Levee) at a banquet at Colosimo's Café. At the head table are Colosimo, John Torrio (called Turio), "Diamond Joe" Esposito, and Mike Merlo. Joe De Andrea was a Colosimo labor racketeer and Harry Cullet was a former policeman who tried to bribe Chicago police in 1914 to take it easy on vice in the Levee. At the time, Detectives Howe and Murphy were the right-hand men of Captain Ryan, who was in charge of the 22nd Street station.

Some of America's finest entertainers graced the stage of Colosimo's. Diners could enjoy the show from their white clothed tables or take a spin on the dance floor. (From the collection of Joe Walters.)

First Ward Aldermen Michael Kenna (front row, second from left) and John Coughlin (front row, third from left) are with what appear to be other faithful members of the Democratic Party at an unidentified location. This is possibly an excursion taken by the Illinois delegation during a political convention. (From the Lawrence J. Gutter Collection of Chicagoana, Special Collections, Richard J. Daley Library, University of Illinois at Chicago.)

William Hale "Big Bill" Thompson, the three term (1915-1923 and 1927-1931) mayor of Chicago, ran a wide-open town, to the benefit of organized crime. Newspaper accounts state that Big Bill's later election campaigns received generous support from Al Capone. Editorials in 1931 in the *Chicago Tribune* and 22 other major American newspapers provided a resoundingly negative assessment of his years in office.

Jake Guzik (left) was at the center of Chicago organized crime for decades. He worked with Jim Colosimo in the glory days of the Levee, with Torrio and Capone during Prohibition, and was one of the most valuable members of the Outfit until his death in 1956.

Harry (left) and Sam (right) Guzik were photographed after their arrest on vice charges. The Guzik brothers were well established vice merchants in the early 1910s and continued on that path until the 1930s.

The Four Deuces, at 2222 S. Wabash, was a Torrio and later a Capone managed vice joint.

Frankie Yale, Al Capone's New York mentor, is wearing clothes that look like they are from the "old country." A very dangerous man, Yale was in Chicago when both Colosimo and O'Banion were killed.

At the start of Prohibition in 1919 authorities dumped this beer into Lake Michigan. Prohibition agents loved to pose for the press while destroying confiscated liquor and equipment. Unfortunately, many of them were corrupt and quite a few of them became bootleggers.

Most Prohibition-Era speakeasies were just pre-Prohibition saloons that remained in business, serving lower quality products provided by whichever gang controlled the area. Some violence has just occurred in this one.

This is a typical illegal distillery, uncovered during a 1925 raid. Given their simple construction and features, stills (and breweries) could be, depending on their size, hidden almost anywhere, such as in a garage, a barn, a basement, a warehouse, or a factory.

John Torrio is seen in January 1925, after he was shot by the Weiss-Moran gang. Torrio taught Capone how to conduct business, including the importance of diplomacy.

Jack McGurn (left), born Vincenzo Gibaldi, was arrested on this occasion with his half-brother, Anthony DeMory (right). Based on the records of the Chicago Crime Commission, McGurn started out with the North Side gang. Although this seems unlikely, it makes considerable sense. His stepfather, Angelo DeMory, was reportedly murdered by Genna gangsters in 1923 and the easiest way to kill the killers was to join the North Siders.

Frank Nitti was Al Capone's first cousin and minded the store in the late 1920s during Capone's frequent absences from Chicago. Throughout his career he was a front office strategist. For example, it is difficult to find any mention in the newspapers of his name in direct connection with violence during Prohibition. Instead, he sent Capone centurions such as Jack McGurn, Claude Maddox, and Rocco De Grazia to handle the heavy work involved in business activities during the Beer Wars. This 1930 mug shot is the earliest known official photo of Nitti and is published here for the first time.

Ralph Pierce was a Capone gunman and protégé of Sam "Golf Bag" Hunt in the 1920s. He later served as Murray Humphrey's bodyguard and eventually became the Outfit gambling boss in the 5th, 6th, and 7th wards. A brainy hood, Pierce was also plenty tough.

Chicago's reform mayor Bill Dever (in the center, shaking hands) is at a public event with Alderman Pat Carr (at the left). A dedicated, honest official, Dever tried to enforce the Prohibition law. He was defeated after one term when the populace returned Thompson to office in 1927. Carr was elected to the very lucrative position of Cook County Sheriff in 1926 only to die before he could take office.

The strip on Cicero's 22nd Street, where Torrio and Capone set up their headquarters in 1924, is buzzing with activity. The Hawthorne Hotel, Hawthorne Smoke Shop, and the Anton Hotel are clearly visible.

Capone (left) and South Side Irish gang leader Ralph Sheldon (right) are enjoying themselves, probably in the mid-1920s before the latter moved to the West Coast because of tuberculosis. This picture was almost certainly taken in Hot Springs, Arkansas, where mock saloons were a common photographer's background scene. Sheldon was convicted of kidnapping in California in 1932 and died in San Quentin in 1944.

Frank Lake, shown here in the mid-1920s, was a major Torrio-Capone ally.

Alleged members of Detroit's Purple Gang are lined up in this Detroit Police Department photo. The Purples had close ties to the Capone gang, supplying them with liquor imported from Canada.

"Bloody" Angelo Genna, perhaps the most fearsome of the Genna brothers, is seated next to a sister-in-law and her child at a Genna family meal.

Joe Saltis (center) was probably leaving court when this photo was taken. Notice the resemblance he bears to the two men with him; if not his bodyguards, they may be his brothers, John and Steve.

Edward "Spike" O'Donnell's mug shot was taken in 1931. At 6 foot 3 inches, and 180 pounds, Spike was a brawler who backed up for no man. His various enemies made numerous attempts on his life and he lost several of his brothers during the Gang Wars, before calling it quits in 1932.

Dion O'Banion was the devil-may-care leader of the North Side gang. Starting as a small time thief and safe cracker, O'Banion, along with Hymie Weiss and George "Bugs" Moran, used his political influence to control Chicago's densely populated and extremely thirsty North Side.

North Side leader George "Bugs" Moran (center) is apparently pleading "no contest" to charges of vagrancy and gun carrying in a Waukegan, Illinois court on October 21, 1930.

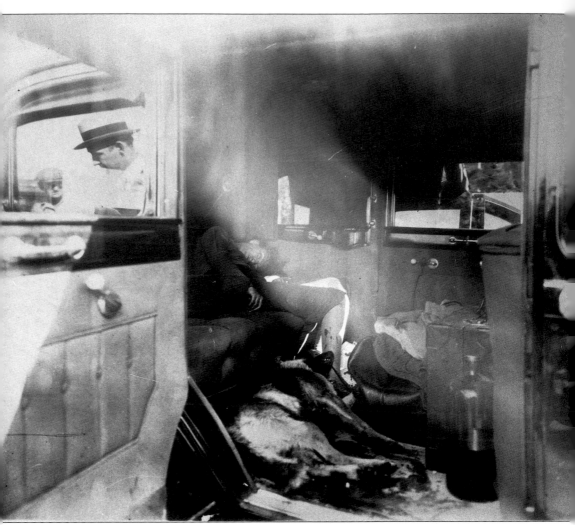

Frank McErlane was the most dangerous man in Cook County, if not the entire United States, during Prohibition. And that was when he was sober. When he was drunk, which appears to have been much of the time, no one was safe—including his common law wife, Marion Miller (also known as Elfrieda Miller, McErlane, or Rigus), and her two dogs. In a fit of rage, McErlane killed all three of them in October 1931.

Two

THE GANG WARS

The Sheldon gang, the Gennas, Druggan and Lake, and the (later on the scene) Guilfoyle (on the Northwest Side, led by Marty Guilfoyle), and Circus (on the near Northwest Side) gangs were Torrio-Capone allies. The North Siders were allied with Matt Kolb and his men (just north of the Guilfoyles and at one time joined with them), north suburban gangsters such as Roger Touhy in Des Plaines, Matt Hoffman in Wilmette, and Ray Pregenzer, who was based near Fox Lake, and had sometime allies in the West Side O'Donnells and the Saltis-McErlane gang. The Saltis crowd and the South Side O'Donnells were, however, mostly independent, immersed during much of Prohibition in a separate struggle for control of the area around the stockyards, which at various times involved the Sheldon gang as well as others.

The south suburbs, centered in Chicago Heights, deserve special mention in any history of organized crime in Chicago. They lined up with Capone in 1926 after he helped a non-Sicilian gang, led by Dominic Roberto and his top aide Jimmy Emery, gain control from the incumbent Sicilians there. The "Heights" was a mecca of illegal stills, referred to in various articles as the most lawless town in Cook County, and this was an understatement. It was the center of the production and distribution of illicit alcohol in the Midwest. The Chicago Heights guys also controlled Joliet as well as most of the area west of Indiana, north of Kankakee, and south of Chicago, providing Capone with substantial income, support and protection along his southern border. When the *Chicago Heights Star* was overly critical of the Heights gangsters, they bombed its offices. The situation in Chicago Heights became so bad that, after the murder of the police chief of neighboring South Chicago Heights, federal authorities took over the town in January 1929, seizing city hall and the police station and raiding a number of locations.

The Beer Wars intensified when John Torrio was shot by avenging North Side gunmen in January 1925. He left Chicago in March of that year and Al Capone succeeded him. After three of the brothers were killed by the North Siders under Earl "Hymie" Weiss in early 1925, the Gennas surrendered. Their rackets were quickly taken over by Capone, who had Tony Lombardo installed as president of the Unione Siciliana, a former Sicilian benevolent organization that now controlled the home production of illegal alcohol. Remnants of the Genna gang set up shop in suburban Melrose Park while other members joined Capone. In 1926, the West Side O'Donnells and the Capone Mob collided over liquor sales in Cicero. The West Siders lost and were absorbed into the Capone gang. As time went on, the Sheldon gang, now led by Danny Stanton, became closely linked with Capone as well.

The gang wars continued for several years, with the North Siders losing Hymie Weiss in October 1926 to gangland bullets and Vincent "Schemer" Drucci in 1927 to a policeman's gun. George "Bugs" Moran then became the leader on the North Side, with Chicago allies such as gamblers Barney Bertsche, Billy Skidmore, and William Johnson, vice czar Jack Zuta and the Aiello Brothers, who ran the Sicilian rackets from Division Street after Lombardo's death. In terms of the number of killings, the gang wars in Chicago peaked in 1926. There were occasional truces, such as the Hotel Sherman treaty in October 1926, but these lasted only briefly, largely because the North Siders tended to disturb the peace. Little changed on the territorial map overall, until after the St. Valentine's Day Massacre in 1929.

The deaths of six Moran men (and the optometrist, Dr. Schwimmer) in the garage at 2122 North Clark Street on the morning of February 14, 1929, and more importantly the killings of Zuta and Joe Aiello by Capone gunmen in 1930, were followed by the fragmentation of the Moran gang and the Capone takeover of the North Side in 1931. Shortly thereafter Capone moved in on the Northwest Side and the northern suburbs, killing Matt Kolb and Matt Hoffman in 1931. At that point the gang wars were essentially over. Bootlegging in Chicago and the vicinity, excluding the Back of the Yards region and the Touhy gang's north suburban interests, were controlled by the "Capone" (Al himself having some trouble with his income taxes) gang and its allies. After Prohibition ended in 1933 and Roger Touhy and several of his men were convicted of the staged kidnapping of Jake Factor in 1934, the Capone crowd reigned supreme.

While they fought over the liquor business during Prohibition, Capone's gang moved heavily into other rackets. These included gambling, labor unions, and business racketeering. Also, the gang's activities spread beyond the city. Unlike beer, which is ready for consumption only days after brewing, many hard liquors improve with age. Therefore, quality liquor, which Chicagoans had a taste for, often came not from the stills in Chicago Heights, on Taylor Street, or on Division Street after sitting for a few days, but from outside the country. And cooperation with Detroit and elsewhere was required to import it from Canada. In return, the local alky was heavily exported, to places such as downstate Illinois, Wisconsin, Kentucky, Iowa, and South Dakota. Beer was wholesaled to other gangs, including those in the Chicago suburbs and other places in Illinois. This contact with other areas provided a foothold for later expansion.

Also during Prohibition, political corruption increased dramatically, as police and officials were paid on an unprecedented scale to look the other way. In fact, as things progressed the gangsters ran many of the politicians. This gave the Capone gang a monopoly on political protection after they gained complete control of the Chicago area. Although Al Capone was shielded by the local authorities, he did not escape the attention of the federal government. He boarded a train for the U.S. Penitentiary in Atlanta in May 1932, just as his underboss, Frank Nitti, returned from prison. Nitti, who was previously the point man on the takeover of the alky rackets such as the Unione Siciliana, succeeded Capone as the demise of Prohibition loomed.

This famous photo of Al Capone, eight top Chicago hoods, a little girl, and a dog was for years a historical mystery. Until recently even the people in it were not correctly identified. From left to right, they are: (front row) Frank LaPorte, Vera Emery, Al Capone, Willie Heeney, and Jimmy Emery; (back row) Rocco DeGrazia, Louis "Little New York" Campagna, Claude "Screwy" Maddox, Jack Heinan (probably), and Sam Costello. (Identifications, except for Jack Heinan, are from an article published by the author and Matt Luzi in *Criminal Organizations* in 1996.) The photo was taken behind Jimmy Emery's house in Chicago Heights, probably in Autumn of 1928. Related photos appear elsewhere in the book.

Jimmy Emery (left), John Roberts (center), and Dominic Roberto (right) are toasting each other in this very early photo, possibly taken before they arrived in the United States. Notice the pointed toes on the shoes, wide, short ties, and the watch chains (and their younger looks and fuller hair, compared to later photos of them in this book). John Roberts was the name commonly used by Dominic's brother, Giovanni Roberto. (From the collection of John Binder and Matt Luzi.)

Dominic Roberto (center) and John Roberts (second from right) are standing behind the house Dominic and the Emery family shared at 2606 Chicago Road in Chicago Heights. Pictured with them are Jimmy Emery (second from the left), his wife Josephine (next to him), their daughter Vera, and their four sons. This house is also pictured in the photo on page 29. Dominic Roberto holds the typical (in gangland photos) place of honor in the center. (From the collection of John Binder and Matt Luzi.)

The Chicago Heights bootleggers gathered en masse—32 men in all—at Nick Neroni's farm, probably in 1926 or 1927 (after the gang wars there ended). This is likely a celebration of the unification of the various factions, all of which are represented here, under Dominic Roberto and Jimmy Emery. Dominic Roberto is again in the center of the photo. The men present, from left to right, are: (front row) Louie Angelotti, "Shebie", George Zeranti, Nick Costello, John Nicastro, Frank LaPorte, and Jim DiPeso; (middle row) James Strangis, Tony Costello, John Roberts, Sam Costello, Pete Zeranti, Dominic Roberto, Charlie Costello, Charlie Presto, Jimmy Emery, Sam Geraci, and Nick DiGiovanni; (back row) Mike Roberts, "Big Jim" Roberts(?), Sebastiano "Curly" Zeranti, Sam LaPorte, J. Pulia, Joe Arrigo, John Perry, Nick Neroni, Joe Guzzino, Sam DiGiovanni, John Piazza, unidentified, Bill Willis, and Tony Sibolis(?). (From the collection of Matt Luzi. Identifications are courtesy of Matt Luzi.)

The backbone of the Chicago Heights Mob relaxes in Hot Springs, Arkansas in a staged souvenir photo. Pictured, from left to right, are Sam DiGiovanni (on the donkey), Dominic Roberto, John Roberts, Tony Costello, and Phil Bacino (on donkey). Charlie Costello is standing in the rear of the wagon. Phil Bacino attended the famous meeting of Sicilian gangsters in Cleveland in 1928 that helped lay the foundation for the national crime syndicate and was active for years in Calumet City. (From the collection of John Binder and Matt Luzi.)

Frank LaPorte and his wife Margaret were photographed together during the 1920s. Although one book claims that LaPorte was Al Capone's boss, there is no convincing evidence to support this assertion. In fact, members of LaPorte's family, who were actively involved in his operations, dismiss this conjecture. Instead, he was a subordinate of Dominic Roberto and Jimmy Emery, who were Capone vassals. (From the collection of John Binder and Matt Luzi.)

Capone hoods Sam "Golf Bag" Hunt (left) and Claude
Maddox (right) are part of this 1930s line-up photo.
Hunt, a native of Birmingham, Alabama, was a top
Capone killer who earned his nickname because on
several occasions police found a shotgun or submachine
gun in his golf bag. Maddox, born John Edward Moore
in St. Louis, Missouri, reached Chicago in the early
1920s. After Willie Heeney's death, he oversaw the
Outfit's operations in Cicero. (From the collection of
the Chicago Crime Commission (CCC).)

"Three Fingered" Jack White (far left), George "Red"
Barker (second from left), and Capone's lawyer Michael
Ahern (with the book) are outside court during Al
Capone's 1926 Prohibition violation case. Barker and
White were with the West Side O'Donnells before that
gang was absorbed by the Capone Mob.

John Scalise (middle) and Albert Anselmi (second from right) are being questioned by detectives after they and Mike Genna shot and killed several policemen on Western Avenue in 1925. Frequently named as gunmen in the killing of Dion O'Banion, they went over to Capone when the Gennas folded. Capone and his men beat them to death with baseball bats in 1929 when they suspected the two of betrayal.

The burial of Angelo Genna at Mt. Carmel cemetery in the Chicago suburb of Hillside was a typical Prohibition-Era gangster funeral. Notice the women in black mourning clothes in the center. Mt Carmel was the hoodlum cemetery of choice. Many of the Italian and Irish Prohibition-Era gangsters are buried there, as well as major figures in the Chicago Outfit.

Al Capone sent this eight-foot floral piece when Unione Siciliana president (and Capone partisan) Tony Lombardo was killed in 1928. Although the murder is usually attributed to the Moran gang, the "word" in the New York underworld and in certain corners of Chicago gangland is that Lombardo was killed by New York gunmen in retaliation for the Capone ordered slaying of his New York mentor Frankie Yale that same year.

The Unione's next president, Pasquale Lolordo, is resting comfortably at home on January 8, 1929, after he was shot by visiting Moran gangsters. The bottles of bourbon and wine that were offered to the guests are visible on the table.

These 1921 model Thompson submachine guns are owned by the Chicago Police Department. The first recorded gangster use of a tommy gun was by Frank McErlane in Chicago in September 1925. New evidence uncovered by the author (from a *Chicago Daily News* article on November 12, 1924) shows that Dion O'Banion brought one to Chicago from Colorado in the fall of 1924; however, he was killed before he got a chance to use it.

This gangster was found in his car with a bullet wound in the head. The real story of Prohibition is that of young men with expensive clothes and automobiles, carrying large rolls of money, who were slain before they reached the age of 30. Often they were murdered by their closest friends for breaking the rules of gangland or because the friends were rewarded by a rival mob they were about to join.

Most gangland killings during Prohibition were quiet affairs, designed to attract as little attention as possible. Many victims were taken for a "one-way" ride in their own vehicle, with a trusted associate sitting in the back seat, as probably happened to this gentleman. When a secluded spot was reached the shooter would kill the victim, often firing through the front seat and using a pistol with a cut-off barrel for ease of pulling and turning in a tight space. The killer would then be picked up by another car waiting nearby.

The killers of this hoodlum ignored the municipality of Chicago's request, shown on the salt box to the left, to help keep the city clean. A "gangster-looking" gentleman, with a light colored coat, dark shirt, and light tie, is standing behind the hood of the car.

This police photo was taken at the scene of a double killing in Chicago during Prohibition. Notice the two hats and the driver's head slightly behind the passenger's. The shooter, who was on the passenger side of the car, given the entry wound on the right side of the passenger's head (next to the ear), probably leaned in the window and shot the man nearest him first and then the driver.

The St. Valentine's Day Massacre, engineered by Al Capone and his ally, Claude Maddox, occurred at the S-M-C Cartage garage on the morning of February 14, 1929. Based on ballistic evidence, circumstantial evidence, information in the New York underworld and a confession by Byron Bolton, the gunmen were Fred "Killer" Burke, Gus Winkler, Ray "Crane Neck" Nugent, Bob Carey, and Fred Goetz, while Byron Bolton was a look-out across the street.

Six men were found dead inside the garage when police and a small army of news photographers arrived. The bodies are (perpendicular to the wall, from the right): Reinhard Schwimmer, John May (in the mechanic's overalls), Adam Heyer, Albert Weinshank, and Peter Gusenberg (on the chair). James Clark (real name, Albert Kachellek) lies parallel to the wall, at the feet of Heyer and Weinshank. Frank Gusenberg has already been removed to the hospital where he would die a short time later.

John May's brains are clearly visible in this photo. According to the coroner's report, only two shot gun shells were fired and May and Schwimmer were each hit in the back by a single blast. Therefore, the upper left side of May's head must have been removed by .45 slugs from the machine guns, as opposed to the often repeated statement that he was hit in the skull by shotgun pellets. In fact, a .45 round was found inside his brain.

This photo was taken from the west end of the garage at 2122 N. Clark. Notice the white carnation (described in the coroner's report) being removed from Reinhard Schwimmer's lapel, perhaps because officials felt it looked unseemly.

A .38 revolver, believed to be Frank Gusenberg's, is clearly visible in the bottom right corner of this photo. An enduring myth about the Massacre is that George Moran only had seven men in his gang. Moran could not have delivered the booze on the North Side, much less have held Capone off for years, with only seven followers. In reality, he had a large, well organized gang that was a force to be reckoned with.

Three

AL CAPONE

Al Capone was born on January 17, 1899, in Brooklyn to respectable and law-abiding Italian immigrant parents, who eventually had a total of seven sons and one daughter. As a youth, Capone was a typical street tough, adept with his fists and part of a local gang. He caught the attention of Frankie Ioele, better known as Frankie Yale, and graduated to organized crime under his tutelage. Yale was the boss of Italian gangland in Brooklyn and also had a dive on Coney Island, where Capone worked as a bartender/bouncer.

At the time, Yale's men were battling the established Irish "White Hand" gang for control of the Brooklyn docks. Soon wanted by the law and the White Handers, Capone was sent off to join Colosimo in Chicago, along with his wife and only child. As was typical of the period, he started at the bottom, as a bouncer at a Torrio run house of prostitution located at 2222 S. Wabash Avenue. From this humble beginning Capone quickly rose through the ranks, running things while Torrio was on vacation in Italy, including the takeover of Cicero in 1924. The bulk of Capone's family later joined him in Chicago, most of his brothers becoming involved in gangland, but only Ralph ever rose anywhere near the higher levels of management.

When Torrio left Chicago during a violent shooting war, he turned over leadership—in return, certainly, for annual cash payments—of Chicago's largest and best organized gang to Capone, all of 26 years old. It was Al Capone's to lead, if he could hold on to it. During the gang wars, Capone showed that he had learned valuable lessons from Torrio, who was a sage in underworld circles. He sought to compromise with foes when possible, rather than always descending to violence, and quickly incorporated allies or defeated enemies, many of whom were non-Italian, into his gang. But continual problems with the Weiss-Drucci-Moran gang led to open conflict and the eventual defeat of the North Siders by Capone and his allies, putting him at the undisputed top of all of Chicago gangland at the age of 32.

Al Capone, however, had little time to enjoy his triumphs. The violence in Chicago during the 1920s, particularly the St. Valentine's Day Massacre, and his own flamboyant, attention seeking style made him a visible target for the law. The federal government moved against him, launching a two-pronged offensive. One prong was an attack on Capone breweries and distilleries by Eliot Ness and other Prohibition agents, which caused the Capone gang some financial damage but never resulted in any major prosecutions. The second prong was an IRS investigation of his income and whether he had paid income taxes. Just as the gang wars were being won, Capone was convicted of income tax evasion in October of 1931.

After serving a few years in Atlanta, Capone was transferred to the new maximum security federal penitentiary on Alcatraz Island in 1934. However, by the late 1930s the syphilis he had contracted in Chicago some time after 1926 had ravaged his mind, incapacitating him to such a degree that he was no longer capable of running a criminal organization. He was paroled in 1939 and joined his family in the house on Miami's Palm Island he had acquired in 1928. Al Capone lived the rest of his life there, in a type of mental limbo—some days lucid, other days incoherent—always accompanied in public by a lawyer or bodyguard, lest he start talking unguardedly.

All in all, Capone's criminal career was an incredible roller coaster ride. Not surprisingly, a number of myths have arisen about him. He has been portrayed in movies and books as middle aged (or older) during Prohibition, excessively violent, or stupid. None of these depictions are correct. Capone was (as already noted) quite young during his time in Chicago, about as violent as your average Prohibition-Era gangster and quite a bit smarter, as evidenced by the fact that he built a criminal empire which was the envy of every other gangster in America. There is also no "lost fortune" to be discovered by treasure hunters or publicity seekers. Amazingly, Capone managed to spend it all during his pre-prison years.

The Lexington Hotel, at 22nd and Michigan, was Capone's headquarters in Chicago starting in 1928. This is how it looked when the Capone hoods had the run of the place. Although years later Geraldo Rivera searched the basement for hidden wealth, the truth is that Capone and his successors kept their assets in banks and real estate and there was no chance that anything of value would be found.

A young Al Capone was picked up on December 26, 1925, by the New York Police for shooting Irish "White Hand" gang members on Christmas Day in what is described as the final battle between them and Frankie Yale's forces for control of the Brooklyn docks.

Capone's Palm Island winter home outside Miami, Florida, became his permanent residence after his release from Alcatraz.

Capone is working out with a bodyguard in Florida around 1930. In some versions of this photo, the other man is identified as boxing champion James Braddock. Braddock, however, stood 6 feet and 3 inches tall (as opposed to the 5-foot-11-inch-Capone) and does not resemble the person in the photo. But, the fellow with Capone is a perfect match for the man in the photo on page 29 who is in the back row, second from the right.

The publicity shy Mae (Mrs. Al) Capone, hiding her face from photographers, sits in the back of a car while visiting her husband at Alcatraz. She remained loyal to him throughout her life, despite his indiscretions and the turmoil of being married to America's most famous gangster.

Albert Francis "Sonny" Capone, the only child of Alphonse and Mae Capone, is playing in a Florida golf tournament as his bodyguard looks on from above. Sonny Capone spent most of his life in Florida, later changing his name and eventually moving to California to be with one of his daughters and her family.

Ralph "Bottles" Capone was arrested in July 1926. His nickname implies beer distribution activities during Prohibition, but Ralph was actually the overseer of all the rackets in Cicero when Al Capone controlled that suburb.

Peggy (the first Mrs. Ralph) Capone graced the newspapers after she was arrested with Ralph in April 1926.

One of Al's six brothers, John, was arrested in 1932 for questioning in a gangland slaying.

Pictured here is Al's brother, Matt Capone, as he appeared in 1950.

Al's brother Umberto "Albert" Capone, shown here in 1960, spent much of his life as a low level Outfit member involved in gambling. His bloodlines brought him little special consideration in an organization that promoted based on merit.

A public relations ploy, Capone's soup kitchen at 935 S. State Street operated from October 1930 to April 1931, just before he struck a deal with the U.S. Attorney's office that would, he thought, settle his income tax evasion case.

This is one of several well-known photos of Al Capone taken at the Chicago Police detective bureau when he was arrested on Feb. 25, 1931.

Capone is pictured here at Comiskey (White Sox) Park on September 9, 1931, attending a Cubs-Sox benefit game for charity where Cubs' catcher Gabby Hartnett signed a baseball for Albert "Sonny" Capone. Seated at the left is Illinois state legislator and later U.S. Congressman Roland Libonati. In the second row, wearing the pearl gray fedoras that were a Capone gang trademark, are various Capone henchmen, including Freddie "the Cowboy" DiGiovanni (smoking a cigarette, behind Capone and to the left) and Jack McGurn (turned around with his left hand inside his suit jacket). The man squinting, in the second row at the left without a jacket or hat, is most likely Sam "Golf Bag" Hunt. Fred DiGiovanni was a Capone killer and bodyguard who was shot and killed in the early 1930s at a Capone affiliated club/casino, the Dells, in north suburban Morton Grove by members of Roger Touhy's gang.

1 9 3 3

Eliot Ness (back row, far right) and the otherwise unidentified Untouchables posed for this photo in 1933. Despite what has been written or depicted in several movies and television shows, Eliot Ness did not "dry up" Chicago or get Capone. A very straightforward account that he prepared of his Prohibition agent days appears to have been embellished by Oscar Fraley, his co-author on *The Untouchables*. The truth was further distorted by Hollywood to the point where even Ness would not recognize himself. For example, a member of the Untouchables, Paul Robsky, noted in an interview that Capone instructed his men to surrender peacefully when a brewery was raided, because there was nothing to be gained by resisting federal agents. Furthermore, the only time that Ness and Capone came face to face was in 1932 when Ness and his men helped guard him until he was safely on the train to prison.

Alexander Jamie, Eliot Ness's much older brother-in-law, was a Prohibition agent and federal investigator. He is shown here with some confiscated gangster toys. Jamie was Ness's connection to high level federal officials, such as U.S. Attorney George E.Q. Johnson, which explains how the very junior Ness was given command of a special squad of Prohibition agents.

Three of the Untouchables are destroying the captured beer after raiding a brewery in Cicero. Although Eliot Ness was a hardworking, honest government agent, he was also a self-promoter with a healthy ego, who limited his own effectiveness by bringing newsmen along on raids.

U.S. Attorney for Northern Illinois, George E.Q. Johnson, accompanied by his wife and son, George Jr., was sworn in as a federal judge on August 17, 1932. Johnson directed the prosecution of Al Capone for income tax evasion and the federal inquiry into the Capone gang's Prohibition violations, the latter resulting in a 5,000 count indictment that never went to trial.

Al Capone originally pleaded guilty to tax evasion, but withdrew his plea when Judge Wilkerson would not be bound by any agreement made by the government. According to the FBI, Murray Humphreys delivered a bribe, most likely to someone in the U.S. Attorney's office, in an attempt to get Capone a light sentence. When word of the deal "leaked" out, Wilkerson refused to participate and the case went to trial.

The Alcatraz Island prison facilities are shown in this aerial photo taken in the 1920s.

Capone is leaving the IRS offices in Florida, with his last lawyer, Abe Teitelbaum, after his tax liabilities were explained to him in February 1941.

Al Capone's casket is being prepared for burial at Mt. Olivet cemetery on Chicago's South Side in 1947. His body was later moved to Mt. Carmel, where the graves of various members of the Capone family can be found.

Four

PROHIBITION ENDS
AND THE OUTFIT BEGINS

Frank Nitti had a difficult job. While Capone inherited a smoothly running gang at the peak of organized crime, Nitti took over in a declining market when there was noticeable external pressure and internal strife. First, the Great Depression hurt gangland's income and the end of Prohibition was about to take away their crown jewel. Second, the Capone gang and its allies were under intense scrutiny, with several top men, including Al Capone and Nitti himself, having been convicted of tax evasion. Third, after the gang wars were over, there was an excess supply of "soldiers," many of whom on the one hand were not good at anything else and on the other hand were not likely to quietly "fade away." A shrinking pie under attack with just as many mouths to feed meant trouble.

The first order of business was to increase the size of the pie. Although this expansion started under Capone, it accelerated under Nitti as Prohibition ended. The movement into new rackets was certainly made easier by the lack of any real opposition after the gang wars ended.

According to Murray Humphreys, Jake Guzik masterminded the move into labor racketeering and gambling. Guzik himself served as the lead man on expansion into gambling while first George "Red" Barker and then Jack White was the point man on taking over the heavily Irish labor unions. After White was killed in 1934, Humphreys, who was active in gambling and hard liquor distribution in "Caponedom," took charge of local labor racketeering. After Prohibition these activities received the Outfit's undivided attention and it soon monopolized gambling in Cook County and the neighboring areas and controlled many of the local unions.

Much of mob run gambling at the time consisted of betting on horse races. Beyond horse racing, there were casino games at various places in the county, such as the Owl Club in Calumet City or in Cicero, and the ubiquitous slot machines, all of which occurred under the blind eyes of various sheriffs of Cook County (of both political persuasions) and other local officials. The Outfit controlled gambling partly by muscling in on the existing operators and partly by expanding what the Capone gang was already involved in so that all operations were either directly Outfit owned or paid a percentage of the profits to them.

Second, Nitti learned the lesson of Al Capone and kept the Outfit out of the spotlight. To quote FBI agent turned author Bill Roemer, they stayed "sub rosa." This was made possible by the post-Prohibition absence of banner headlines in the newspapers reporting spectacular battles over liquor territories. From shortly after the assassination of Mayor Anton Cermak in 1933, to well into the 1940s, the Outfit ran largely unmolested by the law. Many of the local authorities were in their pocket. After Capone's conviction, the federal government moved on to other things, including chasing bank robbers, kidnappers, Communists, and World War II spies and saboteurs. In fact, the Outfit did such a good job of laying low that federal agents, including Eliot Ness, declared the Capone gang finished in 1932 and the FBI, embracing this view,

Jimmy Emery (holding the reins) stands in the winner's circle with his horse Dolly Val on October 24, 1939. The tall man in the rear is Joliet rackets Boss Francis Curry, who was a major Emery lieutenant. Dolly Val could run fast or slow at Emery's command. In one race in 1938 the horse went off at even money but finished so far back there was a track inquiry. Consequently, a week later Dolly Val ran in Detroit at long odds. A surprise winner, at least to the public, it paid $89.80 on a two dollar bet, enriching various people in Chicago Heights. (From the collection of John Binder and Matt Luzi.)

George Moran peaks out from behind his hat after being arrested in Chicago for counterfeiting $200,000 worth of travelers' checks in 1938. Contrary to the impression given by many books, Moran did not leave town after February 14, 1929. In late 1930, he relocated to the north suburban domain of ally Ray Pregenzer and must have made his peace with the Capone Mob shortly thereafter, because he seems to have been in Chicago throughout the 1930s.

The inside of a typical handbook in Chicago (c. 1940) is shown here after a police raid. A dejected sheet writer, with the traditional dark eye shade worn by gambling house employees, sits in front of a police officer. Races at Belmont seem to have been popular with the local bettors.

Charlie Gioe, one of the defendants in the Browne-Bioff case, is waiting outside of court at the time of the trial. Gioe, Paul Ricca, Louis Campagna, Phil D'Andrea, John Roselli, and Frank Maritote were convicted on December 31, 1943, with only Ralph Pierce escaping.

This photo shows Frank Nitti very late in his career. Nitti was in ill health when he took his own life and, according to information in some circles, was suffering from cancer. This helps explain his action, which was rather unusual for a gangster. During that era, many victims of cancer committed suicide rather than live in prolonged pain.

Five

AFTER NITTI

PAUL RICCA AND TONY ACCARDO

The story of the Outfit in the decades after the death of Frank Nitti is, in terms of leadership and method of operation, largely the story of Paul Ricca and Tony Accardo. Paul Ricca was born Felice De Lucia in Naples, Italy, but fled the country when faced with a murder indictment. He entered the United States in 1920 using another man's name and settled in Chicago, where he became commonly known by yet a third surname, Ricca. While working at a Near West Side café—the source of his nickname "the Waiter"— he came to the attention of Frank Nitti, who brought him into the headquarters of the Capone Gang. Ricca spent the rest of the Prohibition Era there, as Nitti's understudy, largely removed from the day to day violence while dealing with the business aspects of gangland. As Nitti rose so did Paul Ricca, becoming his trusted aide and by the mid-1930s the underboss.

Accardo took a different path to the top of gangland. He was born in Chicago, the son of an immigrant Italian shoemaker, and lived as a youth near Grand and Ashland, slightly north and west of the downtown. After a string of teenage arrests for disorderly conduct and auto theft, he graduated to the Circus Gang and then to the Capone Gang proper around 1929. Like many a young hood, Accardo served his time in the trenches, meting out violence and most probably participating in some of the major Prohibition-Era killings as an assistant to Jack McGurn. His nickname "Joe Batters" stems from his ability to use a baseball bat or other blunt instruments on rivals.

Accardo rose fairly quickly through the ranks, from Capone bodyguard and killer in the late 1920s to capo under Nitti to underboss below Ricca after Nitti died. With the hierarchy of the Outfit removed from the scene by the Browne-Bioff convictions, Tony Accardo stepped into the position of acting boss when Ricca went away in 1944. He became permanent boss in 1946, but still regularly visited "the Waiter" in federal prison, by masquerading as Ricca's lawyer, to obtain guidance. Ricca continued to serve as Accardo's advisor and superior after his release in 1947. In the Outfit's setup, Ricca was the "Chairman of the Board" (or Consigliere) and Accardo, the boss at the time, answered to him.

During the Accardo years, although it was already used in the late 1920s by Capone and Bugs Moran to extract money from gambling activities within their spheres, the Outfit widely levied the "street tax" on various criminal activities in Chicago. The operators/perpetrators, even though they did not belong to the Outfit, paid rather than have the Outfit, through obliging politicians, order the police to shut them down. The tax was placed on organized criminal activities, such as gambling in the Chinatown community and elsewhere, as well as on professional robbers and jewel thieves. In some cases this was a simple substitute for Outfit control/operation of a certain racket. If they could not effectively do something or did not want to do it themselves, they would tax it instead.

Gambling provided further opportunities for the Outfit in the 1940s. First, they tightened their control over local gambling, taking over the operations of various individuals, in Lawndale on the West Side and elsewhere, who had previously been paying the street tax. Second, the Outfit muscled in on James Ragen, whose Continental Press supplied racing results to bookies around the country. Ragen fought back with everything he could think of, but was shot in June 1946 and died several weeks later.

Third, a young hood just out of prison with only minor Outfit connections named Sam Giancana came to Accardo in 1944 and proposed the takeover of the numbers game (commonly called "policy") centered in Chicago's black community. Policy gambling was an illegal lottery, similar to the games currently run by the various states, which had prospered for years in Chicago. It had been free from Outfit interference because Al Capone had struck a deal with influential blacks during Prohibition. If they stayed out of bootlegging, Capone would leave gambling in the black neighborhoods alone. With the heat on over Browne-Bioff, and for other reasons, Accardo bided his time. But in 1946 the Outfit went after the policy operators, driving most out of business and taking the games over. The last holdout was tough-as-nails Teddy Roe, who finally succumbed to several shotgun blasts on August 4, 1952.

Ed Kelly (right), Chicago's mayor from 1933 to 1947, is seen here meeting with Bob Hannegan, Franklin Delano Roosevelt's confidante, on August 23, 1944. Murray Humphreys was overheard by an FBI agent in 1961 to say that years earlier he had met directly with Kelly. In return for Humphreys making sure that certain bills passed the state legislature, the mayor allowed Outfit gambling to run wide open throughout Cook County.

Paul "the Waiter" Ricca's Chicago Police Department mug shot was taken on January 24, 1927, when he was arrested as Paul Viela for carrying a concealed weapon. Ricca worked as a waiter/busboy—according to his own account he was the manager—during the 1920s at Diamond Joe Esposito's Bella Napoli café. Rarely if ever mentioned by the newspapers before 1930, he had such a minor official police record that, according to the *Chicago Daily Times*, "it inspired the envy of his gangland associates." He was active in the front offices of the Capone gang, based on Frank Nitti's belief that he was a "good business man". (From the collection of the CCC.)

This image of Tony Accardo is taken from a very early (probably mid-1920s) line-up photo. Although he might never have spent a night in jail due to a criminal conviction, it appears that Accardo was arrested and held overnight at least twice (based on evidence uncovered by organized crime researcher Jeff Thurston).

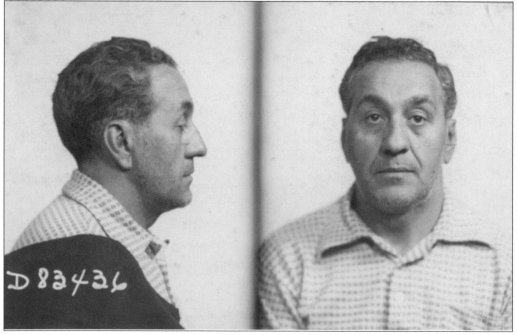

Unusually for a top gangster of this period, Accardo is not wearing a suit or tie in this Chicago Police Department mug shot. He is also sporting what looks to be more than one day's worth of facial hair, indicating that he did spend at least a night in jail on this occasion.

"Tough Tony" Capezio was a leader of the Circus Gang with Claude Maddox during Prohibition and a top Chicago gangster until his death. This Chicago Police Department photo was taken on April 16, 1945.

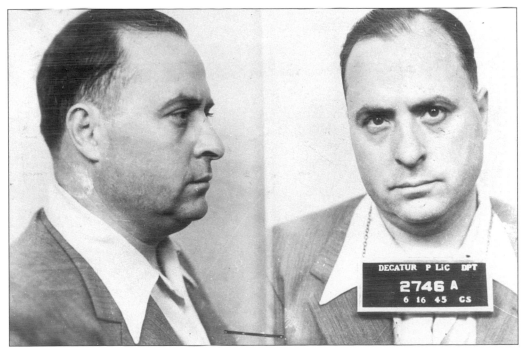

This is perhaps the only photo of Frank LaPorte in the possession of the authorities. LaPorte was arrested briefly on minor charges in Decatur, Illinois, on June 16, 1945, but was quickly released. At that point in time, he was back from duty in the Navy during World War II and was again serving as Jimmy Emery's right-hand man in the south suburbs. (From the collection of the CCC.)

The Chicago Heights guys are seen here enjoying themselves at a cook-out. Pictured, from the right, are Al Pilotto (shirtless), Dominic "Tootsie" Palermo, and Tony Franze. John Roberts is stirring the pot and the shirtless man with his hands at his pockets is most likely Frank LaPorte. (From the collection of John Binder and Matt Luzi.)

Tony Accardo (left) and Sam Giancana (right) were picked up together in 1945. From 1943 to 1978, Accardo lived in three different houses in west suburban River Forest—one a veritable palace at 915 N. Franklin. During much of this period, Giancana lived in neighboring Oak Park.

Jake Guzik was unusually well dressed and looked quite innocent when this photo was taken in July 1946.

Ed "Big Ed" Vogel, who should not be confused with George "Dutch" Vogel, is shown here. The latter was a West Side bootlegger while Eddie Vogel was a Cicero bootlegger and slot machine racketeer during Prohibition. He invited the Torrio-Capone gang into Cicero, at the request of the town's Republican politicians, in return for their help in the 1924 election and they never left. Ed Vogel served for years as the slots and amusement czar for the Chicago Outfit.

Murray "the Camel" Humphreys is consulting with attorneys Mike Brodkin (left) and George Bieber (right) on July 1, 1946. The Chicago Outfit's standard lawyers at the time, they were known as the B&B boys. It is quite likely that they taught Humphreys a thing or two about the law that came in handy during his years as the master fixer for the Outfit.

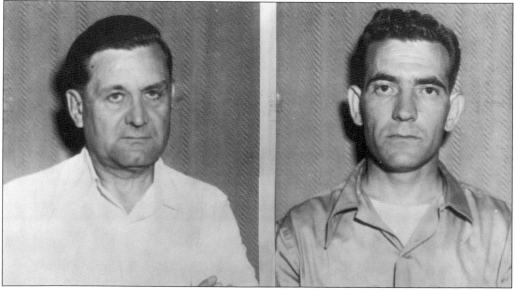

George Moran (left) was photographed in 1946, along with his partner in crime, Virgil Summers (right). Unable to stay on the straight and narrow, by the mid-1940s Moran had reverted to armed robbery. He was convicted and sent to Leavenworth Prison where he died in 1957.

Legendary Chicago burglars and jewel thieves Edward "Butch" Panczko (#5) and Paul "Peanuts" Panczko (#6), were arrested on this occasion with Bruno Scardo (#1), Frank Santora (#2), Fred Petrucci (#3), Charles Szelog (#4), and Steve Tomaras (#7). Burglary gangs such as this one paid the street tax in order to operate.

John Roberts (left) and Frank LaPorte (right) are part of this group photo taken at the Karides studio in Milwaukee, Wisconsin. According to an extremely well-informed source, the man in the center is long-time Milwaukee Mob Boss Frank Balistrieri and the boys are his sons, one of whom was sponsored for First Communion by Frank LaPorte. (From the collection of John Binder and Matt Luzi.)

Paul "the Waiter" Ricca was at the top of organized crime in Chicago from 1943 to his death in 1972. Ricca, like Accardo, lived for years in River Forest. In fact, so many top hoodlums lived there by the early 1960s that even its fine police force referred to the village as "The Home of the Hoods."

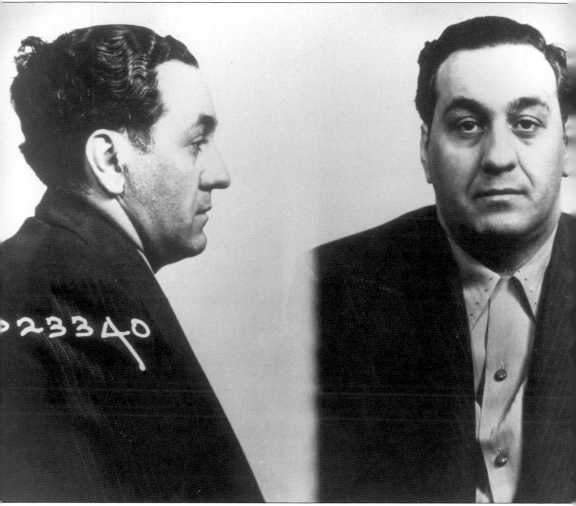

Tony "Joe Batters" Accardo served as the boss or chairman of the board of the Chicago Outfit from 1944 until his death in 1992. He had the longest and most successful career of any U.S. mobster.

Six

THE 1950S

During the 1950s, the Outfit was at its peak. Supreme in Chicago, their gambling and vice activities included clubs and casinos on Rush Street (in the heart of the old North Side cabaret district), in Cicero, and on the Strip in south suburban Calumet City, which was nationally renowned. The Outfit also ran wide open in west suburban Lyons and along Milwaukee Avenue in the suburb of Niles, at the northwest tip of the city, where Eddie Vogel's firm Apex Amusement was located.

Over time, the Mob's vice activities had moved from outright prostitution, because society no longer tolerated visible brothels, to running striptease clubs, with the girls servicing the customers in a less visible fashion. Local gambling included the famous "Floating Crap Game," so-named because its location was changed regularly to avoid detection. Gamblers did not find it, instead they were ferried from downtown hotels by drivers to some nondescript location in the metropolitan area where the game was currently running. Because the Outfit had considerable influence over bars and clubs that used unions they controlled, housed slot machines, or ran a horse racing book, many tavern owners were forced to also use Outfit-owned coin operated machines, such as jukeboxes, cigarette vending machines, and pinball machines. Pinball games provided additional gambling revenue for the Outfit, with the bartender paying off high scores in cash, despite the fact that the machines were supposedly for amusement only.

By the 1950s, the Outfit had considerable "clout" in other cities. It controlled or greatly influenced the crime families in places such as Milwaukee and Madison, Wisconsin, Rockford and Springfield, Illinois, and Kansas City, Missouri, in most cases determining who the leaders were. It also had a major presence in Los Angeles and individual members such as Frank LaPorte had various business activities in California and elsewhere in the West. While it is not true that the Outfit controlled everything west of the Mississippi River, it did have a great deal of power in that area and "spoke for" all the families in the region on the national commission of the Cosa Nostra.

The Outfit's biggest moves in the 1950s concerned casino gambling outside of Chicago. The Outfit first invested in hotel casinos in user-friendly Havana, Cuba. Although somewhat slow to jump in initially, they later went into Las Vegas in a big way and helped build the Vegas Strip. Beginning with the Stardust, by 1961 Chicago had major interests in the Riviera, the Fremont, and the Desert Inn. Their Vegas holdings, partly in cooperation with Moe Dalitz, were overseen by John Roselli, while the submissive Teamsters Central States' Pension Fund provided financing. The Syndicate's revenues in Las Vegas came primarily from skimming the casinos—making sure that significant winnings by the house were never counted as part of net income and taxes on those amounts were never paid.

By definition, when an organization is at its peak, a decline follows. In the case of organized crime in Chicago this decline was caused primarily by the federal government, particularly the FBI. In 1957, the Appalachian meeting of the Cosa Nostra's national commission, a conclave of 50 or more major hoods from around the country called to discuss New York related problems, such as the recent shooting of Frank Costello by Vincent "the Chin" Gigante, was exposed by a New York State Police raid. In response to obvious interstate connections among the crime families in various cities, the FBI instituted the Top Hoodlum Program and devoted massive resources to combating organized crime. Just as Sam "Mooney" Giancana became boss.

During the previous years, Sam Giancana had risen through the Outfit ranks. Tony Accardo recognized him as someone with ideas when he brought the policy racket to his attention. Accardo was Giancana's sponsor when he was "made". Soon he was the driver/bodyguard/lieutenant to Accardo, as indicated by a Chicago Police Department line-up photo of the two of them in 1945. Accardo voluntarily stepped down from the day to day role of boss in 1957, partly to lead a quieter life and partly in response to a federal probe of his income taxes. Giancana, having first learned at the right hand of the master, succeeded him and is believed to have been one of the mob bosses who escaped the police raid at Appalachian by bolting into the surrounding woods. But Accardo remained as the guy who Giancana reported to and who (along with Ricca) counseled him.

The 1950s also saw changes in the upper tiers of the Outfit as a number of the Prohibition-Era hoods who had risen through the ranks over time died of natural causes. For example, Willie Heeney passed away in 1951, Phil D'Andrea in 1952, Louis Campagna and Tony Capezio (of heart attacks) in 1955, Jake Guzik and Sam Hunt in 1956, Jimmy Emery in 1957, and Claude Maddox in 1958. Frank Maritote (aka Frank Diamond) and Charlie Gioe, both of whom had been convicted in the Browne-Bioff case, were not so lucky. They were killed execution style in 1954, as was Bioff himself in 1955 when the Outfit tracked him down in Arizona where he was living under his wife's maiden name, Nelson.

Entertainer Jimmy Durante (seated, far right) and the Chicago Outfit hierarchy are at the Owl Club in Calumet City, probably in the early 1950s. Seated with Durante, from left to right, are Paul Ricca, Louis Campagna, and Frank LaPorte who, along with Tony Accardo, were the club's real owners. Standing at the bar, in the light colored suit and tie, is almost certainly Dominic "Butch" Blasi, who was Accardo's driver and bodyguard at the time. Notice the empty chair at the table, which is probably where Accardo was seated. Blasi would have driven Accardo, Ricca, and Campagna down to Cal City from the western suburbs to see a nationally known entertainer perform at their club. (From the collection of Matt Luzi.)

Jake Guzik is shown after testifying before the Kefauver Committee, which investigated organized crime in the early 1950s.

Ralph Capone (at right) and one-time state senator Dan Serritella (at left), a Capone associate during Prohibition, look quite relaxed on their way to be questioned by the Kefauver Committee.

Pictured, from right to left, are Dominic "Tootsie" Palermo (at the wheel), John Roberts, Jimmy "the Bomber" Catura, Al Pilotto (rear, driver's side), and George "Babe" Tuffanelli. This photo was taken outside the Riptide, a famous spot on the Cal City Strip, probably in the early 1950s. Pilotto and Palermo went on to run the south suburbs for the Chicago Outfit, with Pilotto's brother, Henry, serving as the police chief of Chicago Heights. Tuffanelli, a former sergeant in the Illinois State Police, was later the boss of the rackets in Blue Island. Catura, who was from the south suburbs, got his training during Prohibition from the Capone gang's pineapple expert, James "the Bomber" Belcastro. (From the collection of John Binder and Matt Luzi.)

A Cook County State's Attorney's policeman is at work during a periodic Chicago gambling raid on July 31, 1951. During the Outfit's glory days, infrequent raids were often done for publicity purposes or on independent gambling operations following anonymous tips to authorities from the Outfit itself.

A sizable crowded milled about on Chicago's South Side after Teddy Roe, the last black numbers king, was finally eliminated by the Outfit on August 5, 1952.

While still a young daredevil, Sam "Teets" Battaglia robbed the wife of Mayor William Hale Thompson at gunpoint. Although it is frequently claimed that he started out as a member of the 42 Gang, early newspaper accounts, interviews with 42 gang members by sociologist John Landesco, and a very knowledgeable source consulted by the author indicate that this was not the case.

One of the Outfit's top killers during the 1950s, Felix "Milwaukee Phil" Alderisio did the "heavy work" for years. He later briefly served as the boss of the Outfit.

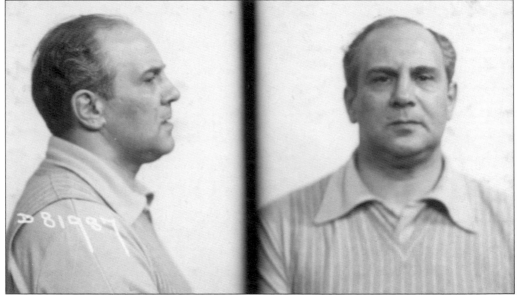

Albert "Obbie" Frabotta, another product of the south suburbs, was Alderisio's first partner on the Outfit's top execution team during the 1950s. Milwaukee Phil eventually found him to be somewhat unreliable and after that paired with Chuck Nicoletti.

Charles "Chuckie" Nicoletti was a top killer for the Outfit who always smiled nicely for the police cameras. When he was a boy, Nicoletti killed his own father, who had attacked Chuck's mother in a drunken rage.

Marshall Caifano was a long-time Giancana associate, going back to their days in the 42 Gang on Taylor Street. He followed John Roselli as Chicago's man in Vegas during their glory years there and, along with Giancana, Alderisio, Humphreys, Chris Petti, Frank "Lefty" Rosenthal, and Tony Spilotro, got himself listed in the Nevada Gaming Commission's "Black Book".

A long-time friend of Sam Giancana, Leonard Gianola was a member of the 42 Gang on Taylor Street during the 1920s. According to one book, Gianola and Giancana were gunmen at the St. Valentine's Day Massacre. In reality, neither was associated with the Capone gang or with the Outfit until much later and Giancana was most likely in jail on February 14, 1929.

Jimmy Emery (at right), late in life, is with a group at the Beachcomber in Miami Beach, Florida. John Roberts is seated across from him (most likely with his wife). Beginning around 1939, Jimmy Emery spent a considerable amount of time in Florida, leaving the day-to-day operations of south suburban gangland to Frank LaPorte. LaPorte became the boss in the south suburbs at Emery's death in 1957. (From the collection of John Binder and Matt Luzi.)

John Roberts (right) is visiting with Dominic Roberto (left) in Italy in 1957. Dominic fled to Italy in 1928 to avoid an indictment and returned in 1931, only to be convicted of perjury. After his release from prison he was deported in 1934. Although Dominic Roberto relinquished control of the Heights area in 1928, he still received a regular stipend from its activities, hand delivered to him in Italy. Also, there were visitors from the U.S., such as Tony Accardo, who met Dominic in Rome in 1959. (From the collection of John Binder and Matt Luzi.)

J. Edgar Hoover is pictured here with FBI agent Tom Bohling, probably at a congressional hearing. Recent claims that the New York Mob had incriminating photos of Hoover and that they blackmailed him to "lay off" organized crime are pure nonsense. If these assertions were true, then why did Hoover come down hard on the Cosa Nostra? And why were the photos never made public?

Accardo invoked the Fifth Amendment 172 times while "testifying" before the McClellan Committee in 1958. Paul Ricca is usually credited with the statement that Accardo had "more brains before breakfast than Al Capone had all day." However, Ricca himself would not have been very far behind in that category, making the two of them among the shrewdest leaders in the history of American organized crime.

Louis Romano (seated at the microphones), a Nitti protege who was president of Local 278 of the Bartenders' Union, told the McClellan Committee "the whole bunch of youse are wrong." As in the Kefauver Hearings, many of America's top hoods appeared and verbally fenced with the senators, but beyond some publicity little actually came of it.

The front steps at 125 N. Lotus in the city's Austin neighborhood are covered with blood after Roger Touhy was hit on December 16, 1959, by shotgun blasts. The shooters were most likely Phil Alderisio and Chuckie Nicoletti. An implacable Outfit foe, Touhy had been released from prison only a short time before. This was one of several gangland killings in the 1950s that showed that the Outfit never forgets.

Seven

THE FEDS
AND THE 1960S

The next decade was not kind to the Outfit. "Free love" cut into the action at their strip joints, with vice becoming less viable and centered on the less visible, high end activities such as call girl rings. Although it took the FBI several years to get up to speed, they quickly came to grips with the Chicago Mob. Bugs were planted in various places the Outfit used for high level meetings. Major Outfit guys were tailed and information about them was gathered in detail. The Bureau even placed Giancana under 24 hour surveillance in 1963, annoying him endlessly. Federal agents made Giancana lose his cool several times, including around his love interest, popular singer and entertainer Phyllis McGuire. They finally granted him immunity, forcing him to testify before a grand jury or be hit with contempt charges. Giancana refused to cooperate and was jailed for a year. Meanwhile, the Justice Department, under Robert Kennedy, made the first moves against corrupt labor unions, investigating the Teamsters Union and its national leader, Jimmy Hoffa, who was convicted of manipulating the pension fund in 1964.

Locally, Richard Ogilvie was elected Cook County Sheriff in 1962 and appointed incorruptible Chicago police officer Art Bilek as Chief of the Sheriff's Police. For the first time in history, the Sheriff's Police conducted major raids on gambling games run by the Outfit, closing casinos, such as the Owl Club, all over the county. Even the Floating Crap game was hit by the Sheriff's Police, at a location in Cicero. At the same time, O.W. Wilson, the progressive superintendent of the Chicago Police Department, did not tolerate visible gambling and vice in the city, moving broadly against these activities. Importantly, Wilson decoupled the police department from politics, changing districts to no longer correspond with ward boundaries and centrally appointing district commanders rather than allowing the ward politicians, who in some cases had strong ties to the Outfit, to name them.

Another factor that hit organized crime was the changing nature of society and politics. During the 1960s, the old style, spittoon kicking, "I'm the boss and what I say goes"-type of politician, one who cooperated with the hoods because that was where the money was, largely disappeared from the political landscape. The new, television covered, "servant of the people" politician was much less friendly to organized crime. Perhaps this was because the public was better informed about mob activities and less tolerant of them. An early example of this change was the election of a reform mayor in Niles who cleaned up the Mob's strip there.

Over time, the pressure, both federal and local, got to Sam Giancana. In return, his erratic behavior and front page lifestyle gave Ricca and Accardo fits. Thoroughly disgusted with Giancana, they deposed him in 1966 and elevated Sam "Teets" Battaglia, a leader of the Battaglia-Carr gang in the early 1930s before joining the Outfit, to the top spot. Sam Giancana wisely left the country for Mexico and points beyond.

Battaglia was not at the helm long, however. The federal government's practice of targeting the top man in the Outfit, which began with Accardo and Giancana, turned the job of boss into a revolving door, with prison on the other side of the door. Battaglia was jailed for racketeering in 1967 and was replaced by Felix "Milwaukee Phil" Alderisio, who was himself convicted in 1969. Long-time Accardo driver and bodyguard Jackie Cerone succeeded Alderisio. In the years that followed, virtually every top mobster in Chicago, including everyone who sat in the boss's chair, was convicted and jailed, with the exception of Tony Accardo.

A new activity that organized crime entered into during the late 1960s was the "chop shop." Chop shops made money through the wholesale theft and chopping up of automobiles, selling the untraceable parts rather than trying to move the entire car. This racket, centered in the south suburbs, was first subjected to the street tax.

Tony "Joe Batters" Accardo is standing outside federal court on November 11, 1960, while the jury deliberates in his income tax evasion case. Accardo was found guilty but the verdict was reversed on appeal, after a number of people from the south suburbs, with connections to Frank LaPorte, testified in ways that helped the defendant. He is shown here wearing the finest Italian silk suit offered by Celano's tailor shop on North Michigan Avenue.

In 1957, Paul Ricca was convicted of using a false name and concealing his criminal record when applying for citizenship and was ordered to be deported. A person can be legally deported, however, only if another country accepts him. In Ricca's case, 52 countries (as of late 1963) refused him permanent entry—largely because "the Waiter" sent the Minister of the Interior of each nation his complete criminal dossier.

Here, Jimmy Hoffa gives Robert F. Kennedy a piece of his mind. As national president of the Teamsters, Hoffa had close ties to organized crime, which dominated a number of the Teamsters locals and therefore the national union as well.

During the mid-1960s, Sam Giancana frequented the Cal-Neva Lodge in Lake Tahoe, Nevada, which was partly owned by his pal Frank Sinatra. One of several Chicago hoods whose name was in the Nevada Gaming Control Board's so-called "black book," Giancana's presence at Cal-Neva got Sinatra in considerable hot water, forcing him to sell his various Nevada gambling interests.

The Rat Pack pose in Las Vegas, in the same order as the names on the sign. The Giancana led Outfit shared girls and good times with Sinatra and his pals. While the others may have used mob connections to advance their careers, Sinatra appears to have been a gangster "wannabe." Among other things, he intimated to Chicago that he could get the Kennedy family to help them out, but did not deliver on that promise.

Sam "Momo" Giancana is in New York in May 1965 for a Grand Jury hearing concerning the disappearance of New York Mob Boss Joe Bonanno.

A top hood by the 1960s, Sam "Teets" Battaglia briefly succeeded Sam Giancana as boss, perhaps partly because Ricca and Accardo were looking for a replacement who was not one of the old 42s brought into the Outfit and advanced by Giancana. In 1967, Battaglia was sent to prison for 15 years for conspiracy to commit extortion. He was paroled in 1973 due to ill health and died not long after being released.

Jackie Cerone is shown here at the age of 39. A top killer and Accardo lieutenant, he later became boss of the Chicago Outfit.

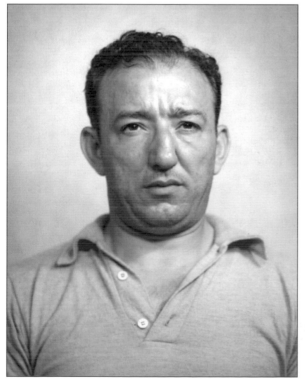

Fiore "Fifi" Buccieri, a feared Outfit killer, was involved in the infamous William "Action" Jackson torture murder in 1961. He was the boss of the near West Side rackets in the 1st, 25th, and 27th Wards during the 1960s.

Rocco Pranno was the vice and gambling boss of near western suburbs such as Melrose Park, Stone Park, Northlake, Franklin Park, and Schiller Park. His cousins served as the police chiefs in Stone Park and Northlake.

Dominick "Bells" Di Bello got his start with Al Capone. He was one of the "Three Doms," along with Dominick Nuccio and Dominick Brancato, who were prominent in Outfit heavy work. He ended his career as the boss of the Near North Side, which included Rush Street.

"Mad Sam" De Stefano, juice lender and torture killer, looks like one of the Blues Brothers in this 1962 photo. The "Mad Hatter" of the Outfit, De Stefano asserted at the time, "I can't prove it, but it's my honest belief that the police have committed 11 recent gangland murders. I know they tried to kill me." In 1964, he offered a South Side newspaper $5,000 to print a regular column written by him, but Sam Giancana cut off De Stefano's literary career before it could proceed any further.

William "Potatoes" Daddano was a Giancana associate and a top 1960s hood. He was active in gambling, juice loans, pinball machines, and jukeboxes. His son, William Jr., is listed by the Chicago Crime Commission as a "made" member of the Outfit and was at one time associated with the mayor of Rosemont, resulting in a recent license application for a casino there to be denied by the state gaming board.

John "John Alcock" Lardino was in charge of the Hotel-Motel Service Workers Union for the Outfit.

An Outfit enforcer and all-around terrorist in the 1960s, Americo De Pietto is one of several Chicago hoods mentioned by official sources as having been involved in some fashion with the narcotics business.

Joseph "Crackers" Mendino was a mid-level hood during the 1960s.

A Cook County Sheriff's policeman is working to suppress gambling on the 22nd Street Strip in Cicero in 1964. The 1920s Capone gang locations are still there, now renamed the Alton Hotel and the Towne Hotel. The old Western Electric plant (22nd Street and Cicero Avenue) is at the far left.

Murray Humphreys was probably waiting outside court in 1965 when this photo was taken. At the time, near the end of his career, Hump was the master fixer for the Chicago Outfit. Along with Nitti, Ricca, Accardo, Guzik, Campagna, and Giancana, he is one of the most important Chicago gangsters in the era after Prohibition. However, recent claims, including that he influenced the 1960 presidential election, are extremely difficult to believe, if for no other reason than the sources, such as his wife, lack credibility. Furthermore, the Outfit would have killed him and her if he even suggested that she be allowed to attend meetings where this (or any other gangland) subject was discussed. As the grandson of one gangster who was close to Al Capone remarked to this author, "I'll tell you one thing. My grandmother never went with my grandfather to any meetings." (From the collection of Ed Baumann.)

Eight

EVOLUTION IN
THE 1970S AND 1980S

Jack Cerone was convicted on gambling charges in May of 1970. In response to the dwindling supply of senior hoods, Accardo formed a threesome, including himself, Gus Alex (real name Alexopolous who is of Greek extraction), and Joey Aiuppa, to run the Outfit, at least until Aiuppa was seasoned enough to be sole boss. Within a few years Aiuppa, another graduate of Prohibition-Era gangland who had previously been in charge of Cicero, held the reins on his own.

The 1970s were tough on the Outfit from a business perspective. Off-track betting cut into their bookmaking operations. The state lottery cut into whatever action there was left in policy and related gaming. And pressure on corrupt unions intensified.

Ethnic change also limited their opportunities in the city of Chicago. During most of the 1960s, the Outfit was active, with the necessary political cover, in every part of the city. A side effect of the Civil Rights Movement, however, was that minority groups elected new people to office who danced to a different tune. As neighborhoods changed, so did the Outfit's ability to function in those areas, with black street gangs openly bucking the Outfit's gambling operations on the South Side. By the 1970s the Outfit's activities were more focused on specific neighborhoods and suburbs where they had influence.

Furthermore, the move into Las Vegas by legitimate operators, including large corporations that started with Howard Hughes in the 1960s, resulted in the sale of many mob-owned casinos. Law abiding individuals and firms, because they had lower costs (relative to the hoods) due to operating efficiencies, found they could run the large Vegas casinos more profitably than the gangsters, even though they paid taxes on all their winnings. While the Outfit was able to cash out during this period rather than being forced out, this still greatly changed the nature of its activities.

But the 1970s were not all bad. With increased interest in professional athletics, bookmaking began to focus on pro-sports, such as football and basketball. The clientele was mostly white and fairly white collar, as opposed to the traditional customers for the numbers or horse racing. Also, the Outfit moved to completely take over the independent chop shops in what became known as the Car Theft Wars in Chicago, with a number of killings as a result. This was only partly successful, given the ease with which independents can steal and dismantle cars.

The 1970s also saw the demise of several major Chicago gangsters. Paul Ricca, who the government endlessly tried to deport because he had lied on his immigration papers years before, died of natural causes in October of 1972. Frank LaPorte, the savvy boss of the south suburbs, also passed away in 1972. Sam Giancana, after returning to the U.S. in 1974, died of unnatural causes in the basement of his Oak Park home on June 19, 1975.

In the 1980s, the Outfit's business activities continued to evolve, while decreasing in size overall. Legal casino gaming cut into mob gambling of all types and by this decade the numbers, betting on horse races, slot machines, and other traditional forms of illegal betting were largely a thing of the past. The Outfit was not completely but at least largely out of Las Vegas by the end of the decade, the process being hastened by federal indictments for skimming in Nevada. Video poker machines in bars, with the bartender paying winners in cash, and professional sports betting, which the Outfit quickly monopolized in the Chicago area by muscling in on the independents, were the two main gambling activities. Juice loans and the related extortion were an ongoing activity, although labor racketeering was rapidly declining in importance due to federal anti-corruption efforts.

In terms of mob leadership, Joey Aiuppa remained at the top during the 1980s, until he was convicted in a Vegas skimming case in 1986 along with Jack Cerone and Joe "the Clown" Lombardo. Joe Ferriola, who had "lined up" independent bookies involved in pro-sports betting during the Aiuppa years as the mob's point man on gambling, replaced Aiuppa as boss. At Ferriola's death in 1989, Sam "Wings" Carlisi took over the top position. Like many of his predecessors, Carlisi had first served as lieutenant to the guy at the top, chauffeuring Joey Aiuppa around and learning by observation. In each case, Accardo served as the Chairman of the Board.

The downsized Outfit reorganized around broad geographical areas in the 1980s. In 1983, for example, the Outfit was believed to be divided into five basic street crews (capos in parentheses) covering the North Side (Vince Solano), the South Suburbs (Albert Tocco), Chinatown (meaning the near South Side base around 26th and Wentworth, which was run by Angelo "the Hook" LaPietra), the West Side (Joey "the Clown" Lombardo), and the Western Suburbs (Joe Ferriola). A separate group, led by Tony Spilotro, oversaw their interests in Las Vegas. By 1990, the Outfit had six, much smaller (in terms of membership) crews: North Side, Chinatown, West Side, Western Suburbs, Grand Avenue, and Lake County. Chris Petti was their man in Vegas at the time, after Tony Spilotro fell into disfavor. Tony Spilotro and his brother Michael were found buried in an Indiana corn field in 1986, having been executed almost certainly by members of the Chicago Heights crew.

The decrease in the number of made members in Chicago was not necessarily a bad thing, although it did reflect a reduction in the scope and nature of their activities. It was likely also a shrewd response by the Outfit to federal inroads and the power of the RICO statute. Less made guys, more associates, meant less guys who could cause real damage if they turned on the Outfit. In fact, to date only two higher level Chicago mobsters, neither of whom were major figures, have been publicly identified as federal informants: Ken Eto in 1983 and Lenny Patrick in 1991.

Joe "Doves" Auippa was at one time the boss of vice and gambling filled Cicero. He went on to become Outfit boss during the 1970s. (From the collection of Wayne Johnson.)

This candid photo shows Gus (known as Shotgun, Slim, or Gussie) Alex later in life. During the 1930s, his family owned a restaurant around 22nd and Wentworth, which was frequented by the Capone Mob, and on at least one occasion they posted some real estate as bond so a Capone hood could make bail. Through this connection, Alex became involved in organized crime.

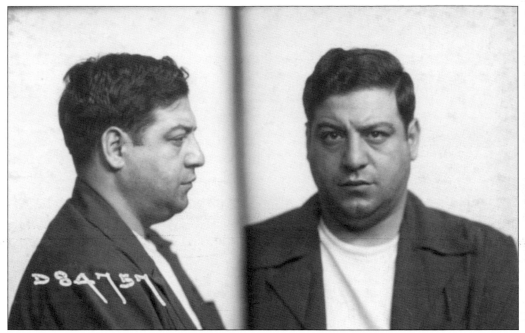

A lieutenant of Sam Battaglia, Sam "Sambo" Cesario was killed (on his own front steps) on the near West Side for fooling around with Phil Alderisio's mistress while he was away in jail. The execution happened after Alderisio's death.

Sam De Stefano, his left arm severed and his heart pierced by shotgun blasts, is lying on the floor of his garage on April 14, 1973. The likely slayers were his own brother Mario, and Tony Spilotro.

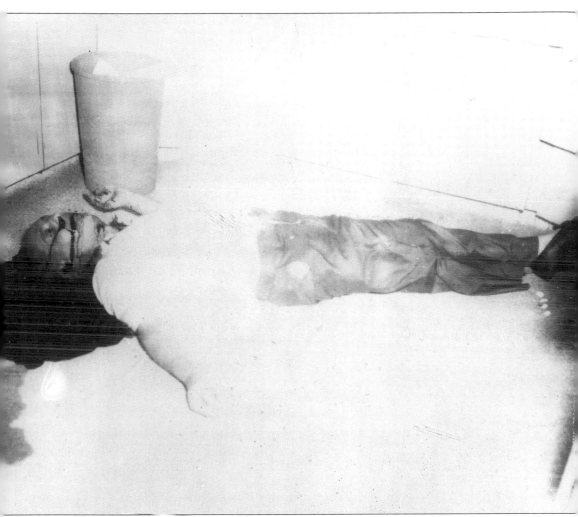

Sam Giancana is lying on the floor of his basement home in Oak Park in a pool of his own blood, after visiting with Butch Blasi.

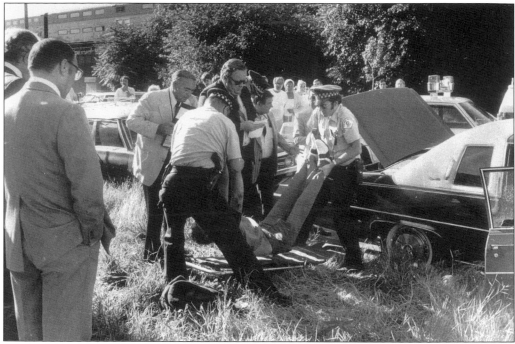

Jimmy "the Bomber" Catura had the difficult task of "lining up" the chop shops for the Outfit. He was killed on July 28, 1978 when his superiors became dissatisfied with his work. (From the collection of Jeff Jabaay.)

James "Turk" Torello was a hijacker and free-lance thief before he joined the Outfit. He ran the western suburbs until his early (natural) death in 1979, which cut short a rising criminal career. This photo was taken in 1954.

William "Billy" Dauber was killed along with his wife while driving in the south suburbs shortly after appearing in court on July 2, 1980. They were casualties in the Car Theft Wars.

Ken "the Jap" Eto oversaw bolita, which is a type of lottery game popular in the Latino community, for the Outfit. This led the newspapers to describe him with the more flattering title "North Side gambling boss" when he turned government informant after a botched attempt on his life on February 10, 1983.

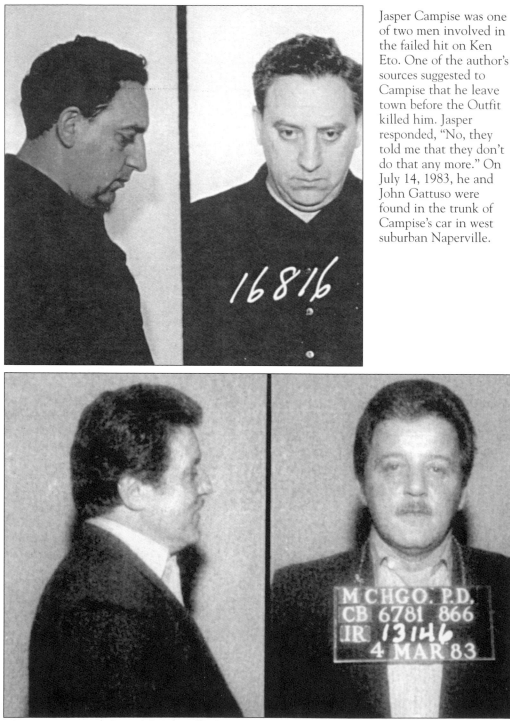

Jasper Campise was one of two men involved in the failed hit on Ken Eto. One of the author's sources suggested to Campise that he leave town before the Outfit killed him. Jasper responded, "No, they told me that they don't do that any more." On July 14, 1983, he and John Gattuso were found in the trunk of Campise's car in west suburban Naperville.

This is a 1983 mug shot of the very flamboyant Tony Spilotro. A killer in his early years with the Outfit, Spilotro went on to be Chicago's emissary in Las Vegas. He seems to have gotten completely out of control while in Las Vegas and may have involved his brother Michael in some activities that his Outfit superiors did not approve of. (From the collection of Wayne Johnson.)

Joe Ferriola was the boss until his death in 1989. At one time he ran the West Side for the Outfit, meaning the area around Taylor Street, which made him the point man on gambling for them. (From the collection of Wayne Johnson.)

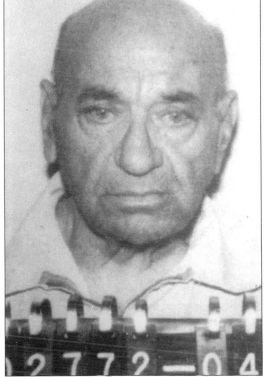

Angelo "the Hook" LaPietra headed the Chinatown crew in the 1980s, which was active in gambling and labor racketeering. He later served as an advisor to John DiFronzo. (From the collection of Wayne Johnson.)

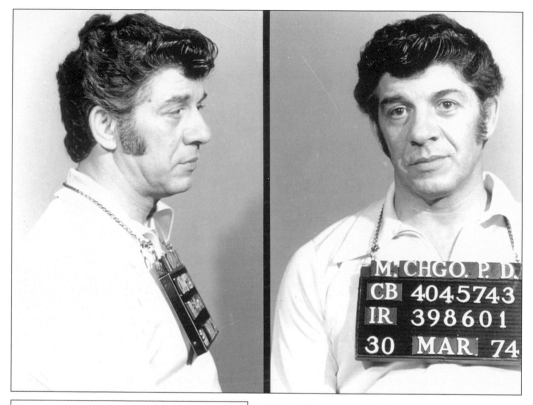

Albert Tocco was the long-time boss of the south suburbs. He was convicted, partly on the testimony of his estranged wife, of extortion, racketeering, and tax evasion in 1989 and sentenced to prison for 200 years. The former Mrs. Tocco also implicated him in the killings of the Spilotro brothers. (From the collection of Wayne Johnson.)

Mob enforcer Frank "the German" Schweihs was involved in gambling and also muscled in on the pornography business. One of the few German Americans active in Chicago organized crime after Prohibition, he was convicted of extortion in 1989. (From the collection of Wayne Johnson.)

Nine

THE 1990S AND BEYOND

The 1990s saw the Outfit retrench itself around sports betting and poker machines. Gone were old time gambling and Las Vegas, most of the labor racketeering, the Strip in Cal City, and the joints in Cicero. Gone was the control of activities in other cities due to federal scrutiny and prosecutions or the disintegration of some Cosa Nostra families elsewhere. Of course, they were ready to do anything that held a percentage for them, such as loot the town of Cicero with the aid of public officials under their control or try to find a way into the legal casinos near Chicago.

One move that boomeranged on the Outfit was a return to 1920s-style extortion, in which they demanded money from people they felt would pay, such as former bookies, with the threat of violence. Perhaps the Outfit's leadership was responding to their decreased business opportunities by becoming more aggressive. In any case, it resulted in wholesale convictions for members of two groups in 1992 and 1993, one led by Sam Carlisi and the other by Gus Alex.

With respect to narcotics, it has been claimed that the Outfit had a long standing policy under Ricca and Accardo that its members were not to traffic in drugs. According to this theory, most of the Outfit's guys stayed away from the narcotics business and those who defied the edict paid with their lives. While there is no evidence of trafficking in narcotics during the Capone-Nitti Era, there are cases during the 1950s and 1960s where prominent Outfit guys were involved in aspects of the drug business, beyond the occasional hijacking of drugs from pharmaceutical firms, without any repercussions.

It appears most likely, in light of these facts, that there has been a prohibition by the Outfit on street level (retail) activity by its members in the sale of drugs, but since about 1950 (or at least at some times after 1950) involvement at the "wholesale" end of the business, such as loaning retail dealers the funds to obtain narcotics or selling them obtained drugs, has been permitted. This would explain the reported executions of some made guys (most likely for retail involvement) while others (operating at the less visible, wholesale level) were not harmed.

Certainly since the early 1990s wholesale trafficking in drugs appears to not be forbidden for made members, but whatever they do is outside of the Outfit. The organization washes its hands of the whole matter, not sharing in the profits, but also not taking any of the risks, including not helping members in legal trouble because of the drug trade.

By the 1990s the Outfit was a shadow of its 1950s stature. In 1997, there were only three street crews. One covered the South Side and the southern suburbs, including activities in Northwest Indiana (basically run from Chinatown by John "Johnny Apes" Monteleone), another handled the West Side and DuPage County (Anthony Centracchio), and the third worked the North Side, Elmwood Park, and the north suburban Lake County areas (Joe "the Builder" Andriacci). These crews may be more fluid than their names indicate, with

111

members moving about the metropolitan area. Recruiting grounds for future Outfit members and associates include gangs of young thieves and burglars centered in Elmwood Park and in-and-around Cicero.

Sam Carlisi was allegedly replaced as boss in the early 1990s by John DiFronzo, but DiFronzo was himself convicted of money laundering in 1993. Since about the mid-1990s, even the best informed authorities have not been sure who was in charge or even if there was a central figure in Chicago. DiFronzo, Joey "the Clown" Lombardo and Joe "the Builder" Andriacci are the individuals most frequently named by official sources as boss, underboss, or consigliere (not necessarily in that order), but there have been a number of conflicting opinions on the subject. The Chicago Crime Commission, for example, named DiFronzo as the boss in 1997 and Lombardo and Angelo LaPietra as consiglieres, but the position of underboss was no longer part of the organizational structure. As this is written, several local sources claim that James Marcello, a Carlisi protege who is currently in prison, is or will soon be the new boss.

Death also took its toll on mob leadership during the years since 1990, rivaling the 1950s as a time when the baton was passed on to another generation. Tony Accardo was removed, after providing leadership during six decades, from the scene in May 1992, something the Feds or the local authorities were never able to do through a criminal conviction. Jack Cerone passed away in 1996, Carlisi died in prison in 1997, as did Gus Alex in 1998, gambling ace Dominic Cortina passed away in 1999, and his close associate Don Angelini followed in 2000, to name a few of the higher level mobsters taken by old age or illness.

Due to a multitude of successful federal prosecutions, the Outfit has again gone "underground," keeping an extremely low profile. This is reminiscent of how they responded to their top leadership being removed in the past—either for income tax evasion or in the Browne-Bioff case. For years during the 1990s there were no likely mob hits, at least until the 1999 shooting of Ron Jarrett (who died in 2000). It was also rumored that street level mobsters were directed not to bother people who did not pay what they owed related to gambling or juice loans. Instead, they were instructed to cut them off from further betting or borrowing.

This low-key approach to crime is possible largely because of the nature of their current main activities. Both sports betting and video poker are eagerly engaged in by the customers and the cash is either paid up front or very likely to be paid, so no coercion by the Outfit is required. Because they currently have a near monopoly on these activities, there is little trouble with competitors. Also, the mob is fairly well insulated from prosecution because the sports betting is done largely by cellular phone, routed through other numbers so that the call is untraceable, and the visible payoff on video poker is done by an employee of the place where the machine is located, not the Outfit.

Given the Outfit's low exposure in these areas and the lack of a clear "victim," the authorities devote little time to combating these activities because the damage they will do to organized crime and the popular support for these efforts are both minimal. In fact, both the Chicago Police Department and the Cook County Sheriff's Police have scaled back their organized crime units and the Chicago Crime Commission has shifted its focus away from the Outfit. For different reasons, but equally to the Outfit's benefit, the federal authorities are currently devoting the bulk of their resources to fighting terrorism and white collar crime. This results in as low a level of interference in the world of Chicago organized crime as has been seen in quite a few years.

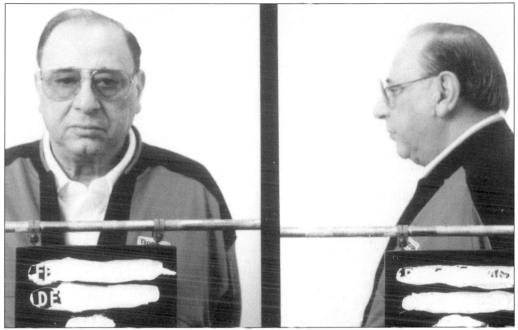

Sam "Wings" Carlisi was once the close confidante of Joe Aiuppa. Although he was Outfit boss from 1989 to about 1992, he was a pale imitation of some of his predecessors. (From the collection of Wayne Johnson.)

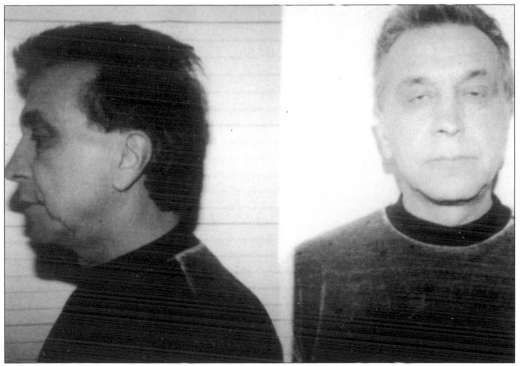

John "No Nose" Di Fronzo succeeded Carlisi and is reputed to be one of the top leaders of the Outfit. (From the collection of Wayne Johnson.)

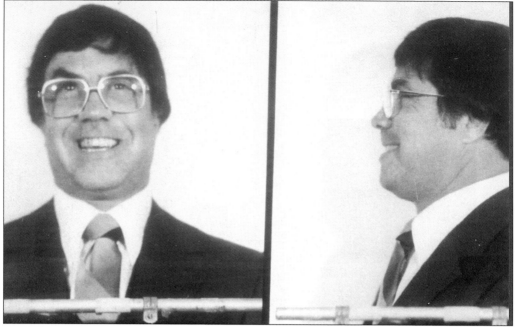

Joey "the Clown" Lombardo has the best sense of humor in organized crime. After his parole in 1992, he took a classified ad in the *Chicago Tribune* requesting that anyone who saw him commit a violation contact his parole officer. According to knowledgeable observers, Lombardo's behavior is a ruse, designed to deceive authorities. He is still believed to be at the top of the Outfit. (From the collection of Wayne Johnson.)

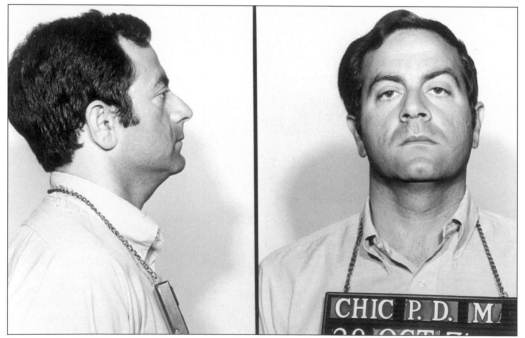

Joe "the Builder" Andriacci is a cousin of Joe Lombardo. He is frequently cited as part of the Outfit's upper leadership. (From the collection of Wayne Johnson.)

Ernest "Rocky" Infelice served during World War II as a paratrooper. He went on to be the underboss before a federal conviction for racketeering removed him from Chicago gangland.

Donald "The Wizard of Odds" Angelini was for years a top guy in gambling. Angelini died in December 2000, depriving the Outfit of one of its more intelligent and capable leaders. (From the collection of Wayne Johnson.)

Dominick "Large" Cortina, a close associate of Don Angelini, was also involved in gambling. (From the collection of Wayne Johnson.)

Leonard "Lenny" Patrick was at one time the gambling boss in the West Side and later, when his constituents moved, North Side Jewish neighborhoods. A killer and extortionist, he is still under federal protection, despite perjuring himself on the witness stand after turning government informant.

A feared mob enforcer, Harry "the Hook" Aleman was tried a second time in 1997 and convicted of the murder of Billy Logan, after it was established that his first trial was fixed and therefore "double jeopardy" did not apply to the retrial. In jail he spends much of his time painting; landscapes are a favorite subject.

Dominick "Tootsie" Palermo succeeded Albert Tocco as mob boss of the south suburbs. (From the collection of Wayne Johnson.)

John "Johnny Apes" Monteleone, now deceased, was at one time the leader of the South Side crew of the Outfit, which now includes the south suburbs and Northwest Indiana. (From the collection of Wayne Johnson.)

James Marcello affects a rather comical pose in this mug shot. He served as the driver for Sam Carlisi and was convicted with him in 1993. (From the collection of Wayne Johnson.)

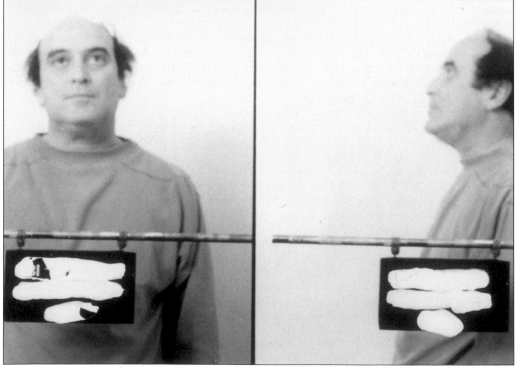

Ten

THE OUTFIT

AN EVALUATION

In the opinion of the author, and the Chicago Crime Commission, the Outfit has been the most successful of the Cosa Nostra crime families. For instance, while some other families have dominated one or a few union locals, Chicago not only controlled many locals but parlayed that into control of regional or national entities. Second, the Outfit has had incredible political influence in the Chicago area. For example, New York's most powerful gangster, Lucky Luciano, was imprisoned for directing prostitution in 1936. Such a conviction would have been unimaginable in Chicago at the time. Similarly, for years the Outfit almost completely controlled suburbs such as Calumet City, Chicago Heights, Cicero, and Stone Park. While this type of power is not unknown in other parts of the country, it is quite rare. Third, although the Outfit's activities have always been heavily centered around Chicago, it has had much greater influence outside its home base than other crime families.

Why has the Outfit been so successful and, relatedly, why have its fortunes declined in recent years? Regarding its great success, first and foremost the Outfit has had excellent (in criminal terms) leadership at the top as well as at the next level. Looking at the bosses from Colosimo through Giancana covers the topic adequately because this was the period of the Outfit's formation and greatest accomplishments.

This group contains Colosimo, who built a modern crime family, Torrio, who astutely refined it, Capone, who made it supreme in Chicago, as well as Nitti, Ricca, Accardo, and Giancana, who repositioned it and directed it into new areas. Several of them had obvious shortcomings. Colosimo's inability to pursue bootlegging, Capone's flamboyant behavior, and even more so Giancana's quickly come to mind. But overall they thought strategically, such as taking over a union local so they could control the national which they used to extort money from Hollywood. In the process they reinvented the Outfit several times, which greatly affected its prosperity. Also, they generally understood when to keep the organization out of the public view. Relatedly, many capable individuals served in subordinate roles, including Campagna, Guzik, and Humphreys.

Second, unlike most other crime families, the Outfit has been multiethnic in nature. This diversity allowed them to tap a much larger pool of talent than elsewhere. It is reflected in the rank and file of the Outfit as well as in the higher level positions, which have been filled at times by people named Guzik, Heeney, Maddox, Hunt, Humphreys, and Alex (who served at the top). Third, there has for years been a large Italian population in the Chicago area, giving the Outfit a strong recruiting base because its membership (though diverse) has been heavily of Italian descent. It also provided them with a useful market, because the Italian community has been fairly willing to accept what they purvey.

Fourth, in Chicago, traditional organized crime has been completely controlled by the Outfit since 1934. Unlike New York City, where there are five families which are not confined to specific geographic areas, there are no jurisdictional disputes in Chicago, much less Byzantine intrigues cutting across family lines caused by the likes of Vito Genovese, Joe Bonanno, or even Carlo Gambino. Instead the Outfit has had no real local competition since the end of Prohibition.

Fifth, there has been no interference in Chicago from nearby cities, as opposed to the New Jersey-Philadelphia area, where New York has considerable influence, and other areas with several cities in close proximity. This has not only kept others out of Chicago, but it has also allowed the Outfit to impose itself on the surrounding area and on other cities as discussed above.

Sixth, what the public will accept from politicians and organized crime is not the same everywhere in the United States. Chicago had more of a "wide open," frontier mentality than its East Coast counterparts and was more corrupt, making it a more fertile ground for organized crime. For example, in most cities during Prohibition if three gangsters were killed at once it was dubbed a "massacre" and the hoodlums were driven out of town. In Chicago, it took seven deaths in one place to arouse the public. This factor can not be over stressed, because it led many Chicagoans for years to view gangland activity as just business as usual.

Seventh, the Outfit has had ample funds at its disposal. While this is an outgrowth of the six preceding factors, this has also given the Chicago Mob an advantage over other Cosa Nostra entities. Unlike legitimate businesses, organized crime can not raise funds in the capital market—it is limited by the wealth of the organization, its members, and the entities it controls. This cash richness allowed the Outfit to easily expand into gambling after Prohibition and into Cuba and Las Vegas, at the invitation of others who were strapped for funds. Eighth, while this may simply reflect the Outfit's accomplishments, there have been fewer turncoats in Chicago than in other cities, where underbosses or (according to the author's sources) the serving boss turned government informant.

Due to these factors, there has been great stability at the top in Chicago—unlike, for example, in New York City—as well as throughout the organization. Only one boss, Jim Colosimo, was deposed from below and no one has ever been overthrown from the outside. Even Sam Giancana lasted 10 years and was ousted from above with a minimum of instability. At the other end of the spectrum, Accardo's nearly 50 years of leadership are virtually unrivaled in the history of the Cosa Nostra.

The Outfit has clearly declined since the 1950s, but so have all the organized crime families. As opposed to St. Louis and Milwaukee, the Outfit is still in business and in good shape. But it has perhaps suffered a greater decline than most of the other families. The reasons for the general deterioration in organized crime are discussed first and then the causes of Chicago's relatively larger decline are examined.

The greatest single factor in the decay of the Cosa Nostra has been the federal government, an opponent that the Outfit et al. could not outspend, outsmart, or corrupt and against whom their local influence was useless. Especially since they have been armed with the RICO statute, the Feds have made great progress against the hoods.

Second, some of their markets have been greatly eroded by the actions of the government. Leaving aside the repeal of Prohibition, state lotteries and legalized casino gambling also directly or indirectly compete with mob run gambling. Third, times (and public attitudes) have changed. Just as the public in most cities no longer tolerates old style machine politics, it is also less tolerant of traditional organized crime, with visible gambling, vice, and violence.

Fourth, ethnic change and associated political change have affected or eliminated some of the old markets. Relatedly, Italian immigration to the United States has decreased greatly since 1920. Fifth, ethnic assimilation has also decreased their pool of recruits. While immigrants with otherwise limited prospects might have been attracted to a life of crime, their children or grandchildren caught up with the native born in terms of legal opportunities and often chose those instead.

Has the Outfit declined more than the average Cosa Nostra family? Not in percentage terms, because in many cities traditional organized crime has completely broken up, but in dollar terms, such as total revenue, they probably have fallen more than the average. Several reasons for this relatively large decrease can be pinpointed. First, the federal government has been unusually successful against the Outfit. While top mobsters have been convicted everywhere, Chicago has had all of its leaders since about 1966, excluding Accardo, sent to prison. This may reflect unusual efforts by agencies such as the FBI. For instance, agents such as Bill Roemer used a variety of highly effective methods that do not seem to have been adopted in other cities. Also, because the Outfit's reach nationally was much broader than the other families, it was likely damaged more by national efforts against organized crime than were its counterparts.

Second, public tolerance has probably changed more in Chicago than elsewhere. Once recognized as the last bastion of machine politics, Chicago has noticeably reformed in that area and the public's attitude toward organized crime has likely changed with it. Third, the city proper has gone through greater ethnic change than other major cities. Also, Italian immigration to Chicago has lagged behind New York, for example, and the children of top Chicago hoods have generally not followed in their fathers' footsteps, unlike in other cities.

Despite the decline in its fortunes, the Outfit is still active. They can still be found in their favorite haunts, but they have a much lower profile. However, the Outfit is ready to move any time it sees an angle for itself, as evidenced by the recent convictions of the mayor of Cicero and six others with Outfit connections for misuse of public funds. The Cicero case indicates that the more things change in Chicago organized crime, the more they stay the same. This is something that would be appreciated by "Big Jim" Colosimo, who would certainly notice how similar the current Outfit is in its scope and structure to the gang that he led before Prohibition.

This 1928 Philadelphia Police Department mug shot, previously unknown and unpublished, is the earliest photo of Benjamin "Bugsy" Siegel. Siegel started out as a young hood in New York during Prohibition in partnership with Meyer Lansky, and is reputed to have been one of the gunmen who killed Joe "the Boss" Masseria in 1931. He went on to "invent" the modern version of Las Vegas, expanding on the ideas of others to build a national tourist attraction with gambling, the Flamingo, in the Nevada desert.

In 1935, Charles "Lucky" Luciano was arrested for questioning in the murder of Bronx gangster Dutch Schultz. Luciano "Americanized" organized crime and was instrumental in the founding of the Cosa Nostra. He ended the position of Boss of Bosses and divided the underworld in New York City into five families which still exist today, including the one he personally led (now called the Genovese family). After serving time in prison in New York, he was deported to Italy where he died in 1962.

Meyer Lansky started during Prohibition as Benny Siegel's partner in a much feared liquor mob in New York City. Graduating beyond the violence, he was a savvy point man for organized crime in gambling in Florida and in Cuba, reportedly greatly enriching himself and his various partners (including the Chicago Outfit).

Vito Genovese was one of the classic schemers in organized crime history. In the 1930s, he ran the New York crime family that is named after him, but fled the country for Italy when he was faced with an indictment. Genovese returned after World War II and, eager to regain control of what he once had, tried to overthrow Frank Costello in 1957. Ultimately Genovese returned to power until he was sent to prison in 1960.

Carlo Gambino (second from left), New Orleans Boss Carlos Marcello (at far right), and his brother Joseph (second from right) are led out of the city jail in handcuffs for arraignment in the care of two quintessential New York City police detectives in September 1966. They were among the thirteen top hoods from New York and elsewhere who were arrested at the La Stella restaurant in Queens at the so-called Little Appalachian underworld conference. Authorities believe that the meeting was held to discuss a successor to the critically-ill Tommy Lucchese.

Tommy Lucchese, who started out as a Prohibition-Era hood, served very effectively from about 1953 until his death in 1967 as the boss of the organization in New York City, which is still commonly referred to as the Lucchese family.

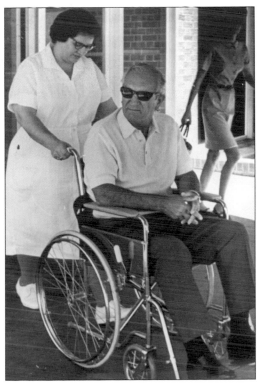

A protege of Salvatore Maranzano, Joe Bonanno was given leadership of Maranzano's family in 1931, which has been known ever since as the Bonanno family. In the early 1960s, his machinations turned other New York bosses against him and he was formally deposed in 1963. He removed himself to Arizona in 1968, where he passed away in May 2002. Bonanno was thoroughly despised by his Outfit contemporaries, especially Tony Accardo.

Joe Colombo (second from right), shown here with his wife, son, and daughter-in-law, led the New York crime family named after him from 1964 to 1971. In an unusual move for a gangster, he founded the Italian-American Civil Rights League to fight the stereotyping of Italians as mobsters and picketed the New York offices of the FBI. Donations to the league were siphoned off by the Colombos.

Vincent "the Chin" Gigante showed no signs of concern when he was questioned in the attempted execution of Frank Costello in 1957. In later years, Gigante ran the Genovese family, sometimes through front men and recently while wandering the streets of New York in his bathrobe in an attempt to convince the authorities that he was a harmless idiot.

Tampa Boss Santo Trafficante had, because of his proximity to Cuba, considerable gambling interests in Havana. He also had close connections to Chicago and is one of the mobsters the CIA tried to enlist in its plot to kill Fidel Castro.

Jimmy "the Weasel" Fratianno had a beard and large eye glasses in 1981 when he was in the federal witness protection program. One of the highest ranking mobsters to turn government informant, he was (according to his own account) the acting boss in Los Angeles at one time. Fratianno dealt frequently with the top guys in the Outfit, given the considerable influence Chicago had in Los Angeles.

SUGGESTED READING

Asbury, Herbert. *Gem of the Prairie*. Garden City Publishing Co., Inc: Garden City, NY, 1942.

Brashler, William. *The Don*. Harper and Row: New York City, NY, 1977.

Demaris, Ovid. *Captive City*. Lyle, Stuart, Inc.: New York City, NY, 1969.

Peterson, Virgil W. *Barbarians in Our Midst*. Little, Brown and Company: Boston, MA, 1952

Roemer, William F., Jr. *Roemer: Man Against the Mob*. Donald I. Fine, Inc.: New York City, NY, 1989.

———. *Accardo: The Genuine Godfather*. Donald I. Fine, Inc.: New York City, NY, 1995.

Schoenberg, Robert. *Mr. Capone*. William Morrow and Company, Inc.: New York City, NY, 1992.

Smith, Alson J. *Syndicate City*. Henry Regnery Company, Chicago, IL, 1954.